How the Wise Decide

How the
Wise
Decide

The Lessons of 21
Extraordinary Leaders

BRYN ZECKHAUSER
AND
AARON SANDOSKI

CROWN
BUSINESS

New York

CROWN BUSINESS is a trademark and CROWN and the Rising Sun
colophon are registered trademarks of Random House, Inc.

Library of Congress Cataloging-in-Publication Data

Zeckhauser, Bryn.
    How the wise decide: the lessons of 21 extraordinary leaders /
Bryn Zeckhauser and Aaron Sandoski.
        p. cm.
    Includes bibliographical references.
    1. Decision making. 2. Thought and thinking. 3. Problem solving.
    I. Sandoski, Aaron. II. Title.
    HD30.23.Z42 2008
    153.8'3—dc22   2008000518

ISBN 978-0-307-33973-7

Printed in the United States of America

Design by Nancy B. Field

10 9 8 7 6 5 4 3 2 1

First Edition

CONTENTS

How the Wise Decide

The 21 Club

To declare war or not to, that was the question.

John Whitehead knew he would have to make a decision soon. His competitors had already made theirs, and Goldman Sachs was coming under increasing pressure to declare its intentions.

For years, Goldman had quietly competed with four other top-tier Wall Street investment banks for the business of America's largest companies. All five banks had been successful enough to make their partners very wealthy.

Then Morgan Stanley fired the first shot in a new kind of warfare, agreeing in July 1974 to help International Nickel Co. launch a hostile takeover bid for Electric Storage Battery.[1] The unthinkable—one company trying to seize the assets of another through financial force—had suddenly become possible. It didn't take long for the fever to become contagious. Corporate executives across the nation were desperate. Many believed they were trapped: Either they took over another company or they faced being taken over. The stakes were enormous, and investment banking clients were willing to pay astronomical fees for help in launching hostile takeovers. Yet amid all the feverish takeover action, the partners at Goldman Sachs could only watch from the sidelines. Whitehead, the cochairman of the firm, hadn't yet given the go-ahead for the firm to advise its own clients on how to launch hostile offers.

Whitehead knew that helping clients make hostile tender offers would be enormously lucrative. And anyone not taking part in the merger mania risked being relegated to the second tier of investment banking. Yet to Whitehead, it didn't seem as if his competitors were really *helping* their clients. Many of the hostile deals were turning out badly for both the acquirer and the target company. The executives at the acquired company often left in anger and the combined company failed to realize the hoped-for benefits of the combination. Whitehead believed it just wasn't good business.

Whitehead made his decision: Goldman Sachs would not offer its services to any company to make a hostile tender offer. He wanted the firm to be known as "the investment bank of integrity."

"We thought that good ethics was good business and that in the end people wanted to deal with the investment banking firm they respected the most, not necessarily the one that was the biggest or had the largest share of the market," he says.

The repercussions of that decision and its public announcement were immediate. A client company turned away from Goldman to retain another firm to help it launch a hostile bid. Goldman's competitors were soon posting record profits on the large transaction fees that flowed from hostile deals. Some Goldman partners argued that the firm was leaving enormous potential profits on the table. Junior bankers watched friends at other banks bringing home big bonus checks. But Whitehead remained steadfast: Goldman was the firm of integrity.

Then something unusual happened. As word of Goldman's stance spread, companies threatened by hostile bids turned to Goldman as the firm of choice to defend against the unfriendly offers. And that prompted executives at companies that weren't threatened to look to Goldman for investment banking advice, too, confident the bank wouldn't turn on them in the future. It didn't happen overnight, but Whitehead's decision to stand firm against making hostile offers set it apart from its competitors and created an enormous demand from companies that wanted to do business with a firm of integrity. Whitehead's decision to eschew hostile takeovers and forgo the lucrative paychecks has become a Wall Street legend. It cost Goldman at first, but eventually created an aura around the firm that has elevated it to preeminence on Wall Street.

Making great decisions isn't easy. Yet the cumulative decisions we make will largely determine our success. The fact that over 80 percent of new products fail after launch and over 50 percent of mergers and acquisitions destroy more value than they create is testament to how difficult it is to make and implement decisions in business today. [2]

In our first jobs as managers, we certainly felt enormous pressure to make great decisions. Yet we also felt unprepared to make them, despite our training at Harvard Business School and McKinsey & Company. How did John Whitehead know to make that legendary decision? We didn't know, but we had a powerful urge to tap into that kind of wisdom. And we weren't alone. Glenn Hubbard, just before becoming dean of Columbia Business School, acknowledged that students at even the best business schools need to better understand the process that will be a critical factor in their future success. "I worry that MBA students here at Columbia, or at Harvard Business School and other good schools, have a great deal of skill mastery and technical mastery, but very little on either identifying opportunity or deciding among alternatives, and those are the things that are probably going to make or break you as a businessperson."[3]

When we couldn't find practical advice on how to make great decisions, we decided to answer a simple question:

How do the really successful leaders make the tough calls?

Our method was straightforward: Go to the source. We would find people who had made great decisions consistently and ask them how they did it. Ask enough successful and experienced leaders about their toughest decisions and surely the essence of decision making would emerge. As it turned out, our first inclination—Go to the Source—became our first principle, confirmed time and again by many of the leaders we interviewed.

This book is the result of our three-year quest to learn how the wise decide. We sat down with some of the world's most talented and experienced leaders to understand how they make decisions. Our research captures the hard-earned lessons shared by twenty-one extraordinary individuals, based on their own most difficult and important decisions. Our wise leaders include John Whitehead of Goldman Sachs; David Maxwell, who is one of two living members of *Fortune* magazine's "The 10 Greatest

CEOs of All Time"; Justice Stephen Breyer of the U.S. Supreme
Court; Stephen Schwarzman, chairman and CEO of The Blackstone Group, the groundbreaking private-equity firm; Harvey
Golub, who was responsible for turning around American Express in the 1990s; and Dermot Dunphy, the remarkable but relatively unknown former chairman and CEO of Sealed Air.

Making great decisions comes down to timeless fundamen-
tals. *How the Wise Decide* distills the six core decision-making principles that our leaders share and that every manager should
know. These principles have guided wise leaders across functions
and industries and brought them through various crises. The six
principles—Go to the Source, Fill a Room with Barbarians, Conquer the Fear of Risk, Make Vision Your Daily Guide, Listen with
Purpose, and Be Transparent—aren't complicated. But as you
will see in the stories of how these leaders made some of their
most critical decisions, it takes extraordinary dedication to these
principles to consistently make great decisions.

You will also see what a powerful force these principles
are for achieving remarkable success. Dermot Dunphy, who you
will watch in these pages transform Sealed Air from a stumbling $5 million packaging company to a $3 billion business on
the cutting edge of technology, calls decision making the "vali-
dation of leadership." As Dunphy explains, "You may have
charisma and personality. People may want to follow you.
But not for long if they realize you're leading them in the wrong
direction."

This isn't a book about business theories. Rather, it is a practical guide written for managers by managers that provides the
advice we all need to make great decisions consistently. Each

chapter explores a single principle that is shared by our leaders. We begin each chapter with a short description of the principle, followed by stories to illustrate wise leaders using the principle to make critical decisions. The insights and nuances that emerge from the case studies are complemented by several practical rules that will help you make the principle part of your everyday decision making. Our goal is to accelerate your journey along the path to wise decision making and successful leadership. In these demanding times, when choosing the right direction is critical, you now can turn to the principles at the heart of *How the Wise Decide.*

CHAPTER 1

Go to the Source

Remember the game you played in kindergarten in which the class, one by one, passed on a whispered statement? When the last child told out loud what she had heard, it was nothing like what the first kid had whispered.

If you're like most people, you're playing a variation of that game every day at the office. Sure, you get authoritative-looking reports to read and you sit through detailed PowerPoint presentations. But you're still getting the same kind of distorted and incomplete information that you got from your classmates in the kindergarten game. That doesn't mean the information you get in the office isn't useful. But you're not going to the source to get *firsthand* information, far and away the *best* kind of information. You may argue that you get out of the office occasionally to meet with customers or suppliers to learn what they're thinking, but that isn't what we mean by going to the source. Going to the source is the relentless pursuit of information from the field. It is hard work, and it takes a lot of time, effort, and imagination.

Do you devote two-thirds of your work time to going to the

source? As CEO of Medtronic, Bill George did. That's how he got a bloody catheter thrown at him in an operating room and solved a serious problem confronting his company.

Do you make more than four hundred customer visits each year? That's how Mike Ruettgers discovered deep in the bowels of a customer's data processing center the need for a new product that revolutionized EMC's fortunes.

Do you travel the world studying how your business thrives in radically different environments? Orin Smith found the solution to expanding Starbucks into untapped markets tucked away in small towns in New Zealand.

All three of these successful former CEOs share a passion for developing primary sources of information. It is one of the characteristics that defined their success. They went places other CEOs didn't and heard things others couldn't. They asked a lot of questions and listened carefully to the answers. They not only got the best information, they also got it faster than anyone else. They were able to use that information to make important decisions about how to beat competitors to market with new products, how to solve critical problems, and what sweeping organizational changes to make for profitable growth. For them, going to the source became a powerful competitive advantage.

But how can Mike Ruettgers make four hundred customer calls in a year? How can Bill George spend two-thirds of his time observing complex surgery in an operating theater or talking to Medtronic employees about developing new products or solving problems? The answer is that they value primary sources of information enough that they make going to them both a priority and a routine. Among all the things a CEO can be doing, they have decided that the largest portion of their time is best spent gathering unfiltered, unbiased information. Other tasks can be delegated, but firsthand observation and conversation require you to be where the action is, whether it's an operating room or your own factory floor.

Making important decisions can be stressful. Information may be skimpy, confusing, or contradictory, especially if it comes to us filtered and diluted through the mind-sets of people who think differently than we do. Wise leaders know that they can never have *all* the information they want. That's why it is critical to have the *right* information. They know that primary information gives them three major advantages over other kinds of data in reaching a decision.

First, information at the source is *unfiltered* by others. Organizations invariably edit and distill information as it moves from level to level and from one department to another. The result is a presentation or a report that purports to capture the essence of a problem, but that may miss or misinterpret some crucial piece of information. Decision makers need to supplement this diet with unfiltered data, information straight from the source that hasn't been manipulated or interpreted.

Second, information at the source provides *subtle details and nuances* that get lost in second- or thirdhand accounts. Reports and canned presentations lack emotional content, but the fact is that emotions play a large role in business. Without emotion, we can't appreciate the passion of a high-potential customer or the frustration of an underfunded product development team. It's the decision maker's job to understand what emotions are at play and to use that understanding to make the best possible decision.

Without face-to-face encounters with the people driving the future of your business, you will miss out on the power of emotional input.

Finally, information from the source is critical because it shows us *reality*. Too often, secondhand information distorts reality enough to give us a false sense of confidence. Only when we see things firsthand—how our product performs, what motivates our employees, what a customer *really* needs to do his job—do we have the breadth and depth of information to make the right decision. Comparing what we have personally seen and heard at the source to all that other information also allows us to put the secondary information in its proper context. The result is better decisions.

Primary sources are all around you, but you have to think differently about who they are. Going to see your customer is a vital part of learning how your product or service is used and how it can be improved. But most customer calls involve peer-to-peer contact. CEOs visit CEOs and salespeople visit purchasing agents. That's the wrong mix. To get the most useful primary information, you have to penetrate much more deeply into your customers' organizations to discover the nitty-gritty details about what people on the firing line want from a supplier. The vice president of purchasing for a big hospital has never used a medical device in surgery, but surgeons have—and they have strong opinions. Similarly, a chief information officer isn't likely to have the same perspective on technology needs as the harried manager of one of the company's data processing centers.

Start looking for primary sources where it's easiest to find them—in your own company. If you're in sales, for example, when was the last time you visited the credit department to check up on your customers' credit ratings and how they've changed over time? Is product development working on something that might benefit from some input from your customers?

Outside your company, there is a vast array of potential sources of firsthand information beyond your customers. Think about potential new customers. And what about your customer's customers? Suppliers and competitors can be good sources of primary information, as are government regulators, investors, news reporters who cover your industry, and academics who study it.

Making it a routine part of your job to go to the source will require a new mind-set, a realignment of your priorities and the tenacity to pursue firsthand information wherever it may take you. But if you become as skilled at using this powerful tool as the three leaders you're about to meet, you can beat competitors, find new markets, and generate terrific new product ideas.

THE BLOODY CATHETER

It was turning into a long, frustrating day for Bill George as he cooled his heels in the corridors of New York City's massive Lenox Hill Hospital. George, recently appointed the president and chief operating officer of Medtronic, Inc., a Minneapolis medical equipment manufacturer, was spending his first ninety days on the job learning about his company's products firsthand in the operating room. But today's procedure, an angioplasty using one of Medtronic's balloon catheters, had been delayed for hours while technicians scrambled to repair the fluoroscope that would show the doctor the route to guide the small balloon into the patient's clogged arteries. The gruff German-American cardiologist that George would observe was furious that his busy schedule was being disrupted.

Finally, the fluoroscope was fixed and the operation could begin. George, gowned and gloved, stood a few steps back from the operating table where the patient lay swathed in sterile sheeting. But soon after the doctor inserted the balloon catheter into the patient's femoral artery, the device fell apart in his hands. Ever so carefully, the surgeon withdrew the catheter from the patient. Then, with ill-concealed rage, he hurled the bloody device at George, who ducked just in time to avoid being smacked in the face. The operation resumed, this time with a competitor's catheter.

George had been aware that Medtronic's catheter sales weren't what they should have been. The company was losing market share and the sales force had been complaining about product quality. But the engineers had said the product was fine and getting better. Maybe the sales force was just looking for an excuse for not doing a good job, he had thought. Now, shaken by what he had just seen, George sat down with the Medtronic sales rep who had been with him in the operating room. The rep told him that the problem he had just witnessed wasn't an isolated incident. The catheters had been failing with disturbing frequency. All the sales reps knew that, he said, and they had all filed the required company reports.

But George hadn't known it, and he wanted to know why he hadn't known it. When he returned to his office in Minneapolis, he began investigating how information about the catheters got reported to headquarters. What he found was a tortuous path that routed the sales reps' reports about failing catheters through seven layers of bureaucracy before they reached the people who designed the products. When George questioned the engineers about the reports, they denied that any design flaws existed and blamed the cardiologists for misusing the equipment.

His investigation of the catheter failure led George to two conclusions. First, there clearly was a problem with the quality of the catheters. He had seen the problem with his own eyes, had been shocked by the incident, and had even brought the ruined device back to headquarters in his baggage.

"It's an overstatement, but field reports are a dime a dozen," George says. "There's no emotional association with them. But when you're in a medical environment like an operating room, all your senses—sight, sound, smell, taste—are working. It's a totally different experience than reading a field report."

Second, and more important, there was something dangerously wrong with Medtronic's ability to handle critical information. "It was a systemic problem," he explains. "What was wrong was that the system wasn't getting quality information from the operating room to engineering, quality control, and manufacturing, the people who could fix the problems. People don't want to pass on bad news, and engineers can be in denial about a problem."

George immediately ordered up a solution to the systemic problem. Within a few months, the catheter sales force was split off from Medtronic's centralized sales operation and attached to the catheter division, where salespeople were in much closer contact with engineering, quality control, and manufacturing. At the same time, George ordered engineers to get out of their offices and spend at least one day a month in operating rooms observing how the equipment they designed was used. A few engineers complained to him that they were too busy to waste time watching doctors. "I said, 'If that's the case, you're working on the wrong things.'"

George calls his traumatic experience in the Lenox Hill operating room a "power-of-one" observation. That single catheter failure crystallized the problem confronting Medtronic in a way that no report ever could. But George wasn't basing his decision to overhaul the catheter business on that one experience. Instead, he was considering it in the context of everything else he knew about the business. He was able to see not only the flaws in the catheter, but also the flaws in how Medtronic handled information.

Other power-of-one observations sparked more changes at Medtronic. One day, George was watching a surgeon implanting an early version of Medtronic's defibrillator, a device that restores normal rhythm to a wildly beating heart. The device was large and the electrodes were delicate. The surgeon was having difficulty fitting the defibrillator into the patient's chest cavity. Finally, he pushed hard, and suddenly blood was everywhere. The surgeon had perforated an artery.

"Surgeons are good at cutting, but they're strong, both in personality and in physical strength. He was trying to force the device when what was needed was the refined touch of a cardiologist," George says. The patient survived, but Medtronic's technicians began focusing on making smaller defibrillators that cardiologists could easily implant without having to do deeply invasive surgery.

Then there was the day George spent in Loma Linda Hospital's pacemaker follow-up clinic, where patients with recently implanted pacemakers come to make sure they're working properly. George hadn't understood at first why the cardiologists at Loma Linda insisted he spend several hours in the cramped offices. What he observed was mass confusion. Each brand of pacemaker and each model required a different monitoring instrument. Which brand and model did this patient have? Where's the monitor for that one?

"It was crazy," he says. He returned to headquarters and told his technical staff what he had witnessed. They immediately set out to develop a universal monitor that could be used with any Medtronic pacemaker or defibrillator in existence or yet to be developed. "I didn't conceptualize it, I just brought back the information and they took it and ran with it. The result was totally transformative," he says.

As the leader of a technologically sophisticated manufacturing company that literally saves lives every day, Bill George used power-of-one observations to make critical decisions about the products that are Medtronic's lifeblood. Those observations showed him not only how to fix faulty products, but also a faulty organization, and they gave him the insights that spurred the development of new products before competitors saw the potential. George went to primary sources time and time again because he knew he didn't have enough information from other sources to make those decisions intelligently.

"At lower levels, common decisions come down to following a set of rules. Things are quantifiable and you need to know what the numbers are telling you," he says. "But the higher up you go and the more important the decisions become, the more those decisions depend on power-of-one observations. You take away a lot of unquantifiable impressions that way, whether you're in the retail business visiting stores or you're in the automotive industry noticing how different cars handle."

George's power-of-one observations certainly paid off handsomely for Medtronic. During his twelve years of leadership from 1989 to 2001, the company's market capitalization soared from $1.1 billion to $60 billion, averaging 35 percent growth per year.[1]

MR. SMITH COMES TO TOWN

When Orin Smith joined Starbucks as chief financial officer in 1990, the company was on a roll. Howard Schultz, the CEO, was driving the growth and expansion of the company at a furious pace, inundating major metropolitan areas with outlets that featured the best coffee, the friendliest baristas, and impeccable service. Consumers loved it. The dense populations of cities such as New York, Seattle, and Chicago made it economically feasible to open multiple outlets, some within a few hundred feet of one another, despite the fact that each outlet's main product cost only a few bucks.

Ten years later, when Smith succeeded Schultz in the top job, prospects weren't looking so bright. Sure, the company now had 2,135 locations and was expanding into major foreign cities, but it seemed to some business analysts that Starbucks had saturated the major metro markets in the United States.[2] At corporate headquarters, many of Starbucks' managers did not believe it was possible to continue to increase the annual number of new store openings and were pessimistic about sustaining the company's growth. Poor Orin. It looked as if he would be the fall guy, the CEO who presided over the decline of Starbucks and the fall of its high-flying stock price. A reporter from *Newsweek* summed up the situation: "After a decade of phenomenal growth in its North American café business, Starbucks now has to figure out an Act II." [3]

Which is precisely what Smith set out to do. Smith not only believed Starbucks was far from saturating major metropolitan areas, but also asserted that there were many new opportunities as well. Smith, who had grown up in Chehalis, Washington, a small town about a hundred miles south of Seattle, had long harbored the notion that Starbucks needn't be confined to big cities, although he didn't deny that the company's operational strategy— a district supervisor overseeing a multitude of outlets—lent itself mostly to big cities, where a supervisor's travel time between stores was minimal. In addition to small towns, he also saw unfulfilled opportunities in nontraditional places like lobbies of major office buildings, off-highway locations, and stores within other large retailers. He believed that pioneering those kinds of new territories would be an important part of maintaining a high level of new store openings and the profitability Starbucks' shareholders had come to expect. He was particularly intrigued with the thought of opening stores in places such as Las Cruces, New Mexico, and Sioux Falls, South Dakota, the kinds of small towns in which he had spent his childhood.

Long before becoming CEO, Smith had explained his thinking to Schultz, a true visionary who believed in the potential for Starbucks more than anyone. But neither Schultz nor most of the management team shared Smith's confidence that annual store openings could be increased. Midlevel managers argued first that it would be too costly to oversee stores in remote locations. Either supervisors would be spread too thinly, spending too much time on the road, or the company would have to hire a lot more supervisors, each of whom would oversee only a few stores. It would also be difficult to supply remote stores with fresh bakery products. More to the point, though, management simply didn't think there were enough people in small towns willing to plop down $3 for a cup of coffee, no matter how good it tasted.

When Smith took over as CEO in 2000, he knew he faced an uphill battle. "In 2000, we had people who believed that our rate of growth had to fall dramatically because they didn't think we could open more than 425 stores a year," he says. "Growth has got to come down. And inevitably it will. You can't grow in perpetuity at 25 percent. There's a time when you have to face that, and say, no, that's the way it is. But I didn't believe we were there."

In a sense, Smith wanted to go back to the future. "When I was growing up and I went into town on a Saturday, the streets were full of people," he says. "I can go back to those same [small] towns now and there's nobody in the street, despite the fact that the population is bigger. Where do they all go? They don't have anyplace to go anymore. The places where people used to congregate and talk with their neighbors don't exist anymore. I figured that we could provide those places."

Smith wasn't just imagining that Starbucks would be welcomed in small towns. For years, he had been talking to people who lived in small towns. Once they knew he was a Starbucks executive, they wanted him to open a store in their town. Every time Smith went back to Chehalis during his tenure as Starbucks' CFO, his old friends and neighbors would ask him when the town would get its own Starbucks. A few of his friends even pressed him to give them a franchise for Chehalis.

Then there were the letters. Hundreds of them. They came from all over America, written by small-town mayors, chambers of commerce, and ordinary residents of rural areas. People from small towns were traveling more, and when they came across a Starbucks in their travels, they loved it. They wanted one at home, and they took the time to write letters to Starbucks begging the company to open a store where they lived.

Requests from friends in his hometown for a Starbucks franchise and letters from small-town mayors weren't statistically calibrated market data, just emotional appeals from people who wanted a Starbucks near them. But the outpouring from all those potential customers was enough to convince Smith long before he became CEO that the demand for Starbucks' unique blend of coffee and hospitality was there in thousands of small towns across the country. As a result, he wasn't interested in hearing from the staff that Starbucks would have to cut back store openings. He wanted to *accelerate* them.

Yet the operating staff wasn't just imagining that remote stores would be difficult to run profitably. As Starbucks was growing through the 1990s, the group that finds new locations had taken it upon itself to open a few stores in small communities near Spokane, Washington. The experiment seemed to prove their point. Sales were great, an indication that consumers loved having a Starbucks in their town. But the stores weren't very profitable, the result of just the kind of costly management and logistical issues that the staff had said the company would encounter in small towns. When Smith pressed them to analyze the small-town market, they came back with a gloomy prediction: Only five hundred to a thousand small towns had the demographics that would support a Starbucks store.

Smith didn't believe it. He had heard from too many people in too many little towns to think the market was that small. "The staff was using the same demographics that we had in the metropolitan areas to make their estimate," he says. "I thought their estimates fell far short of the possibilities." Nevertheless, Smith didn't press his case. He admitted to himself that unless the company could surmount the logistical and management hurdles facing small-town operations, it wouldn't make sense to move ahead.

Then Smith took a fateful trip to New Zealand. It wasn't anything special, just one of the typical journeys senior Starbucks executives routinely made to check out how the company's foreign operations were doing. The New Zealand operation was a joint venture between a franchiser and Starbucks. Smith first met with the franchiser's staff in Auckland, a big city in its own right. Then, just as he does anytime he leaves headquarters, Smith wanted to visit some stores. Visiting stores to see how employees and customers are taking in the Starbucks experience is like oxygen to Smith and other senior executives. They crave the experience and won't be denied it. They want to talk to people, ask questions, learn what's right as well as what's wrong. And, of course, they always have a cup of coffee during the visit. It's an occupational hazard.

"I'll typically visit six or eight stores a day when I'm not in the office," says Smith. "I love the product, so I'll have a cup at every store. But I don't finish them. I have to throw some out each time when I'm leaving. Otherwise, I'd get wired pretty quickly."

But visiting stores in New Zealand wasn't the same thing as visiting stores in New York. As he and a handful of New Zealand executives drove along narrow two-lane roads passing hills, crops, and hundreds upon hundreds of sheep, Smith realized that in New Zealand Starbucks was very much a rural operation. After hours on the road they would pull up to a local Starbucks in a town of five thousand or so people with only a block or two of storefronts, mostly small stores selling the kinds of things farmers routinely needed. Inside the Starbucks store, he invariably found happy customers. He also found the solution to managing rural stores.

In small towns in New Zealand, the lack of other opportunities made a Starbucks store manager's job one of the best to be had. People competed to get the jobs, intent on making it their career. The franchiser was able to hire older store managers, many of whom already had retail experience and who could manage people. They didn't need a district manager looking over their shoulder every few days to be sure they were doing everything the Starbucks way. Turnover of both managers and staff was exceptionally low. What's more, these stores had solved the logistical problem of having fresh food in the stores by sourcing it locally from bakers.

It was close to an epiphany for Smith: Here's how you run rural stores! He already knew the demand was there in small towns, and now he knew how to manage the stores he so badly wanted to put in those small towns.

Smith brought his insights back to headquarters and put a

team to work to figure out the logistics of distributing fresh product to stores located many miles away from big cities. At first, they came back with the same answer that Smith had found in New Zealand: local sourcing. But with some more investigation, they found an even better solution: a flash-freezing process that allowed a regional bakery already serving metro stores to ship frozen products to stores many miles away. Once thawed in the store, the food was as good as fresh. The solution made perfect sense. Real estate in small towns was much-less expensive than in major metro areas and the company could afford to build bigger storerooms with freezers in rural locations.

With that, Starbucks was ready for the national rollout of what it calls "new market stores." Just as in New Zealand, the manager's jobs in small-town stores were coveted positions that attracted older, more-experienced people who needed much-less supervision by district managers. The flash-freezing process provided fresh food in each store. The company began opening hundreds of new market stores each year and reveling in the reception they got. Las Cruces and Sioux Falls were two of the top performers. Smith's hometown of Chehalis has its own Starbucks today, and, sure enough, it has become a meeting place for townspeople. Smith, who is helping replace the community's hundred-year-old library, finds himself meeting with other restoration workers at the downtown Starbucks each time he goes back.

"There's no place that we have such an enthusiastic response as we've had in small communities," he says. "We're finding things like a community of twenty-five thousand people that ten years ago we would say, 'We're not going to have stores in a place like that,' and today we have three stores there. And guess what? There are lots and lots of communities around the U.S. that have twenty-five thousand people, so the market possibilities just explode."

With his company's future growth on the line, Orin Smith recognized that market reports, analysts' projections, and internal advice weren't enough. He knew with a certainty based on going to the source—conversations with and letters from people in small towns—that there was a vast untapped market that wanted Starbucks. They weren't Starbucks customers, but they wanted to be. That part of the market growth equation was rock solid. What he lacked was the solution to the logistical and management problems. Going to a different source was the only way to get it. Because he was open to and constantly looking for new information, he found that solution in New Zealand. He hadn't been looking for it there, but had he not made that trip to that particular source, the solution might have eluded him completely.

RUETTGERS SPEEDS PAST IBM

Wow, thought Mike Ruettgers, this guy is *really* unhappy.

Ruettgers, the CEO of information infrastructure powerhouse EMC through most of the 1990s, was sitting across from the chief information officer of Deere & Co. in the CIO's expansive corner office, listening to a tale of woe.

"It is bad enough to have to try to fix systems scattered across the company that we would never have installed had they called us, but then to be held accountable for systems I didn't even know existed really irritates the hell out of me," said the red-faced CIO, the veins in his temples bulging. "Now, after crashing my entire organization, they're all coming to me telling me I've got to take over running and maintaining their data processing because they can't handle it. I told them not to do it in the first place, and now they want me to take over this mess. The only way I'll take these things back is if they crawl on their hands and knees over a hundred yards of broken glass!"

Ruettgers had been hearing similar complaints from other CIOs for the past few months, but none were this vociferous. It was the 1990s, and the use of computers was exploding throughout industry. Every department in every company wanted dedicated hardware and software. If the IT departments couldn't keep up with the demand, individual departments and business units took it upon themselves to create the systems they wanted, often without consulting the beleaguered IT department.

But few department heads anticipated the problems that came with their own data systems. They had to be staffed twenty-four hours a day and, more important, when something went wrong, there seldom was anyone in the department who could fix it. That's when the department called either IT or the CEO. If IT got the call, the technology specialists often found themselves confronted by a cobbled-together system using different hardware and software than the company's data center used. It took much longer to figure out what had gone wrong and fix it. If the CEO got the call, it wouldn't be long before he was on the phone to the CIO wanting to know what the hell was going wrong with the company's information technology department.

It sounded to Ruettgers as if Deere's CIO was fed up and wasn't going to take it anymore. Somewhat taken aback by the CIO's emotional outburst, Ruettgers offered sympathetic comments. But at the same time, he was firming up the outlines of a new business for his company.

"I had seen bits and pieces that indicated distributed or department data processing was coming back to the main data centers, but there wasn't any research or anything else that said, you know, 60 percent of it would be back in the next five years," Ruettgers recalls. "I had asked if he had seen any of that happening, and that question allowed him to articulate all the problems that he was having as a CIO as a result of this. I talked to a lot of customers, and the conversations would be useful, but not always particularly important. So when somebody reacts so emotionally, you know he has to be pretty deeply invested in what's going on. I knew that if he has this problem, other people are going to have the same problem. The key would be to develop a solution and get it into the market faster than anyone else. If we could do that, then we would own a major new transition that was beginning to take place."

What if, Ruettgers thought, there was a device that could bridge the different data processing systems in a company like Deere and let them talk to the same storage system? Wouldn't that really simplify life for guys like the Deere CIO?

Nothing like that existed at the time—not from IBM, not from Hitachi, and not from EMC—and nobody seemed particularly interested in creating it until the idea coalesced in Ruettger's mind. In fact, when he took his idea back to EMC, his senior managers weren't enthusiastic. Business was just fine, they said. The company didn't need to be spending money and effort chasing a product for which there wasn't a clear demand. Engineers working on EMC's profitable mainframe storage products had absolutely no interest in seeing resources diverted from their projects. The sales force was very content to keep pumping out more of the products that were earning their quarterly bonuses.

"I had some supporters, but if you had taken a company-wide referendum on this idea I had, it would not have passed because we were doing so well on the mainframe side," Ruettgers says. "We had gone from zero market share to 35 percent and were expecting to be at half the market the following year. We were gaining share, we were growing like crazy, everybody was doing well, and the customers were very happy. Nobody saw any need to move into what I call the open-system side, or the client-server side. But I was convinced that this transition was taking place kind of behind the scenes, and I wanted to get ahead of it because I always thought that if you get to the market first, typically you get most of the market share."

Undaunted by the internal resistance, Ruettgers told EMC's board of directors that he intended to create a new division to work on the development of a device that would allow different computers using different software to communicate with a single storage system. "They said, 'Mike, if you want to try it, go ahead,' " he says.

Ruettgers recruited an outsider to run the division since EMC didn't have that expertise in-house. Many of the 250 engineers who eventually wound up working on the development of the device came from outside as well. Ruettgers believed that creating a new division and keeping the development separate from EMC's successful ongoing business ensured that the new project wouldn't get lost.

In June 1995, after eighteen months and about $50 million, EMC introduced the Symmetrix 3000, which worked with a wide variety of server computers and enabled users to consolidate their open systems information in a single, powerful, intelligent storage system. Sure enough, EMC caught its chief competitors, IBM and Hitachi, flat-footed. Hitachi immediately began development of a similar product, while IBM, apparently not believing the market would be big enough or lucrative enough, held back temporarily. And at first, it looked as if IBM might be right. Ruettgers was confident enough about the Symmetrix 3000 that he set ambitious goals for sales, captured in the slogan 2-4-8, which stood for $200 million in Symmetrix 3000 sales the first year, $400 million the second year, and $800 million the third year. Yet at the end of the first quarter of sales, the company had posted only $15 million of sales against a $25 million target.

"One of the things that happens when you set goals is that a lot of people react differently," says Ruettgers. "If you set a goal of, say, making ten putts in a row from five feet, some people might think, 'Yes, I can do that,' but if they wind up making just five putts, they'll say, 'That's pretty good.' Only a few would say, 'You know, I really need to make all ten.' "

One attractive feature of the Symmetrix 3000 was its small size. One person could carry the device in its carton. After he received the first-quarter sales report, Ruettgers spent most of a night stacking unsold cartons of Symmetrix 3000s in salespeople's offices. It was his way of letting them know that he was serious about achieving the sales goals he had laid out. The message got through, and the sales force buckled down to moving the hardware. In the first year, sales of Symmetrix hit the $200 million target; and by the fourth year, sales were approaching $2 billion, constituting over half of EMC's revenues.

Mike Ruettgers's seminal idea and his decision to pursue the Symmetrix 3000 seem to have grown directly out of his conversation with an upset CIO at Deere & Co. But in reality, it came out of the four hundred to five hundred customer visits he did each year as CEO of EMC. Many of the visits produced only bits and pieces of information. But when a catalyst came along like the emotional rant of the Deere CIO, all those bits and pieces suddenly became a coherent map that showed the way for a new product that revolutionized data processing and storage. It took Hitachi a little over two years to bring a similar product to market, and a skeptical IBM took even longer.

"You're able to do a tremendous amount of primary research when you visit customers," Ruettgers says. "Research on this industry is probably about twelve months old when it's published, so you're not likely to find anything new coming out of the research houses. When you're trying to pick up early indicators of what's going on, you have to pick it up firsthand."

The creation of the Symmetrix 3000 is one example of just how valuable it can be to go to the source for firsthand information. Ruettgers saw a market developing before anyone else did and moved swiftly to take advantage of that knowledge. But that achievement pales beside EMC's performance during Ruettgers's era in the 1990s. An investor putting $1,000 into both Microsoft and EMC on January 1, 1990, would have found that by January 1, 2000, the investment in Microsoft would be worth $96,000. The EMC investment would be worth $806,000.[4] Going to the source can pay huge dividends.

RULES FOR GOING TO THE SOURCE

Bill George, Orin Smith, and Mike Ruettgers are exemplars of the value of going to the source. Their devotion to the quest for firsthand information sets them apart from most people who feel inundated by meetings, e-mails, internal memos, and Power-Point presentations. They produced the kind of market and financial successes that clearly establish the value of going to the source. Where do I find the time to go to the source? you may well ask. Follow our wise leaders' examples and the time will create itself. Once you realize how valuable it is to go to the source, you'll find opportunities to do it more often than you imagined possible.

Rule #1: Make It Routine

Going to the source isn't about one seminal visit to the operating room or one trip to a small town. Bill George and Orin Smith made vital discoveries during a single visit to an operating room and a single trip to New Zealand, respectively, but those discoveries were made because both leaders were able to put their observations in context. They used their personal experiences in the operating room and in New Zealand to calibrate the rest of the data they had, both from inside their companies and from many other observations outside the walls of their offices. Bill George knew that Medtronic catheters were a problem, but he hadn't experienced the extent of the problem until he ducked the bloody catheter. Orin Smith knew small towns wanted Starbucks stores, but he also knew it would be difficult to manage and serve stores in small towns. He recognized the solution to meeting untapped demand in small towns in New Zealand because his mind was tuned to linking together disparate pieces of information.

Making a routine of going to the source takes time. At the beginning of each year, Bill George blocked out large chunks of time on his schedule that he knew he wanted to devote to going to the source. He didn't always know in advance just where he would go or who he would see, but the time was reserved and the rest of his schedule was built around those blocks of time. George traveled extensively to seek out sources, often combining a visit to a Medtronic facility somewhere in the world with meetings with doctors and observations in operating rooms.

Some of the time he blocked out was committed far in advance to such big events as the American Heart Association annual meeting, a convocation that draws thousands of cardiologists, surgeons, and other specialists. George wouldn't hole up in a luxurious hotel suite to meet with a few select customers. Instead, he spent hour after hour on his feet, either in Medtronic's exhibitor's booth or walking the nearby aisles to be available to physicians who might be upset about something or have an idea for a new product.

Spending time with employees included not only formal meetings at Medtronic facilities around the world, but also informal strolls through offices and labs. One day, George was walking through a lab when some researchers eagerly beckoned to him. They had just gotten permission from the Federal Communications Commission to use a tiny slice of the radio frequency spectrum for a new device that would pick up information transmitted from a miniature computer implanted in a person's body—for example, a defibrillator that stops erratic heartbeats. The FCC permission was the last hurdle they had to clear before the product could go commercial. When George told Medtronic's business planners about the breakthrough, they were unimpressed. It would be too costly and too risky, they said. But George had seen the excitement in the eyes of the researchers and knew they were confident they had a winner. Today, the technology is used to transmit information from patients at home to their doctors' offices over the Internet and is a huge success.

To spend all that time with doctors and Medtronic's employees, George necessarily didn't do some of the things that CEOs who aren't so devoted to getting firsthand information do. To do that, he formed an office of the chief executive that included himself, vice chairman Glen Nelson, a physician with keen business skills, and chief operating officer Art Collins, recruited from Abbott Labs. His two colleagues took some of the burden of the CEO's job on their own shoulders. But George also freed up some time for himself by cutting back on things such as budget meetings.

"If you let yourself, you can do budgets and expenses until the cows come home," he says. "But that isn't where you make money. Our business is based on developing new products. You make money by tapping your customers and your employees for great new ideas and then implementing them."

Developing a routine for going to the source is all about discipline. You need to wander the halls of your own office to talk to people with whom you don't ordinarily come into contact, you need to schedule blocks of time in advance, and you need to make going to the source part of any trips you take.

If, like Bill George, you schedule time for going to the source far enough in advance, you can plan the rest of your schedule around those times with minimal disruption. You may not know when you schedule it how you'll use each chunk of time. You can decide that when the time comes closer. If you're in marketing, for example, you may decide to spend two or three days observing how different retailers advertise and display your products. If you're planning to attend a trade or professional organization meeting, make your trip count. Lectures and seminars are fine— some of the panelists may be great sources—but be sure to carve out time to meet new people who might have useful insights.

But don't restrict yourself to prescheduled times for going to the source. Orin Smith's assistants knew that every time he left the office on a business trip he would want to visit half a dozen or more Starbucks wherever he was going. You can do the same thing by making it a point every time you leave the office to find a source to visit.

Rule #2: Develop Permanent Sources

Developing new sources of information is an important part of going to the source. But it is equally important to cultivate permanent contacts, people to whom you return time after time to be able to read the changing levels of joy, frustration, or demand. Contact with permanent sources—people you trust to be observant and honest with you—may reveal little or no change for a long period of time. Then comes that day when something different catches your attention. Your source may not even realize that she's acting differently or saying things you haven't heard before. But if you're alert to those subtle signals, you'll know to probe more deeply to find the root cause of the change.

One of the pioneers of America's electronics industry, Paul Galvin, a true entrepreneur and thinker, employed this technique for years. Galvin founded Galvin Manufacturing Corporation in 1928 to make simple electrical devices. He soon branched out to manufacture radios for automobiles and eventually changed the company's name to Motorola, reflecting the focus on motorcars and music (Victrola). As Motorola grew, Galvin made it a point to keep his fingers on the pulse of not only the market, but also his own company. He would frequently walk through the manufacturing area, where he eventually met Motorola's first female assembly line worker, Mary Quliza. Bob Galvin, who ultimately succeeded his father as CEO of Motorola, recalls that Mary worked in Department Five, the coil-winding area. Each time Paul Galvin passed Mary's line, he would stop at her station to ask how she was doing. Usually, Mary would greet Paul with a cheerful hello and say that she was doing fine and the job was going well. But sometimes, Mary made it clear that things weren't going so well. While respectful, she would nevertheless tell Paul that the policy he had announced last week wasn't something that she thought was a good idea. Paul knew that if Mary didn't think the policy was a good idea, neither did most of her colleagues on the assembly line. That would set him to reconsidering the wisdom of the policy, and sometimes he would order that it be changed over the objections of other executives, who knew Mary was the source of Paul's change of mind.

"He didn't have to go ask one hundred people," Bob Galvin recalls. "He'd walk up to his office and he'd bring the big shots in, and he would say, 'That decision I announced last Thursday, I'm going to have to change it. The people in the factory don't like it.' "

Paul Galvin's regular visits to Mary and others were a permanent link to his employees. He was at the source looking for power-of-one observations that could tell him when things were off.

Like Mary, people in your own company can be valuable permanent sources. But keep in mind that meeting with other people in your company, especially those at much lower levels, can be disruptive if you're perceived to be treading on someone else's turf or looking to undermine others. Among Orin Smith's permanent sources of information about what was happening in Starbucks stores were the baristas who manned the front lines. Smith created a process that he called "skip levels," in which he would get a conference room in a hotel in whatever town he was visiting and invite some baristas to meet with him *without* their boss.

Smith would ask the baristas what the company could be doing better and what they thought was really going well. Virtually every such session would turn up little things that someone back at headquarters needed to look into. But occasionally, a skip level meeting could lead to big changes. Starbucks began selling merchandise in its stores as another source of revenue and profits, but the concept didn't go over very well with customers at first. When Smith brought up the lousy results from merchandising at a skip level meeting, one bold barista spoke up.

"Nobody ever asks us what we think would sell in the stores," she said. "When we get the boxes of stuff we open them up and just laugh because we know it won't sell."

"It was humorous on one level, but it was sad on another level," Smith recalls. "The merchandizing people weren't talking to our field people about what to sell. A consequence of that skip level meeting is that merchandising now discusses with field people what they'll be selling."

Ordinarily, a boss excluded from a meeting between his employees and someone from headquarters wouldn't be very happy about it. But Smith institutionalized the skip level meetings so that it wasn't at all unusual. And he made it a point never to chastise a boss about anything he learned from the baristas. Store managers learned not to worry about their workers meeting with the Big Boss because the sessions were explicitly *not* about finding out what was wrong so that someone would get called on the carpet.

"I didn't come back and whip my people for having overlooked something," he says. "That wasn't the purpose. The purpose was to learn and change what we could and to make a better decision next time. I just wanted to cut through the filtering the organizational structure always does—not because people try to keep things secret, it's just what organizations do. If I really want to understand what's happening, I have to talk to people who are down there doing things. Otherwise, I'll wind up making poorer decisions, and my subordinates will make poorer decisions."

Smith encouraged other managers to do skip levels and they rapidly caught on. "They don't like me coming in and telling them what I discovered," he laughs. "They would rather discover it first."

You can develop permanent sources both inside and outside

your company. Within your own company, you can find useful sources among people with whom you aren't in regular contact, especially in functions different from your own. If you're a salesperson, make contact with a product engineer. Conversely, if you're a product engineer, reach out to a salesperson. You'll both be better for it, and so will your company.

Rule #3: Find Out Who's Driving

Going to the source is most effective when you go to the *right* source. That may sound obvious, but it wasn't apparent to Starbucks' operations and real estate staffs that the right source was people in small towns. All they wanted to do was look at the demographics of Starbucks' metro customers and apply that standard to the rest of the country. Orin Smith knew better. He was looking ahead to the future to see who would be driving Starbucks' growth, and he had found those potential customers in small towns. He knew that customers outside of major cities were going to be the drivers of Starbucks' future.

Ironically, it can be most difficult to understand who is driving the future of your organization when business is at its best. John Whitehead was cochairman of Goldman Sachs in the late 1970s and early 1980s when the investment bank was enormously profitable and one of the preeminent investment banks in the nation. Its clientele included the biggest and best American companies. But Whitehead was worried. Among the big-five investment banks, Goldman was the only one without an international presence in financial centers such as London and Tokyo. Yet the firm's clients were increasingly doing business abroad. Indeed, as early as 1967, before Whitehead had become cochairman, General Electric, one of Goldman's most important clients, had told the firm that it would be working with Goldman's archrival Morgan Stanley to do a Eurobond issue because Goldman didn't have an international presence.

Whitehead had considered the GE call a dark day for Goldman and began immediately pressing the firm to go international. The customers who had driven Goldman's very profitable rise to the top of the investment banking business were now showing the way abroad. It was up to Whitehead to go where his customers led. But Whitehead's other partners weren't concerned. They wanted to use the firm's prestige and skills to win even more market share in the United States. Trying to go abroad would not only divert capital, both financial and intellectual, from that goal, but it would also put Goldman into competition with formidable banks on their home turf.

"We were so self-satisfied with the success of our domestic business and we were growing so fast that everybody said, 'Whitehead, you're rocking the boat. International, leave that to others.' "

When Whitehead became cochairman, Goldman's international presence was almost nonexistent. But in his powerful new role, he pushed to set up overseas offices, beginning in London. The going was tough, though, and the London office, the sole component of the nascent international division, lost money in its first few years, not an uncommon event when an investment bank enters new turf. There were still powerful opponents among Goldman's partners who opposed the international moves and used the losses as a weapon to bludgeon Whitehead.

"People would tell me that I was blowing serious money on

the London venture and that if this were an office in Chicago or Los Angeles that we'd fire the manager and close it down," Whitehead remembers.[5]

But Whitehead believed he had no choice but to press ahead with foreign operations, so he devised a subterfuge: He eliminated the international division as a separate profit center. From that point on, each domestic division of Goldman—investment banking, trading, equity sales—would absorb the appropriate losses from the international operations. The losses, of course, would simply disappear among the burgeoning domestic profits of each division.

"It was a little sneaky, but it worked very well, far better than I had ever anticipated," Whitehead says. "Other people were eager now to get on board because the division heads wanted to make it profitable and invested more time, money and people in making it profitable."[6]

Today, Goldman Sachs not only has a global presence in investment banking, but in many big markets it is also the kingpin of investment banks, besting such formidable institutions as Deutsche Bank on its home turf in Germany. And it's all because John Whitehead paid close attention to the companies that used Goldman as an investment bank. It took him a while to overcome internal resistance, but he knew from Goldman's clients that the investment banking business was going global with or without Goldman Sachs. "Internationalization was probably a risky thing, but there was no alternative," he says. "We might not succeed at it, but we had to try to do it. If we hadn't done it, Goldman Sachs really would have been more or less out of business, because now all investment banking business is international."[7]

To figure out who is driving your company now and who may be driving it in the future, make a list. Start with the people with whom you interact regularly now. Add to that list each of those people's boss and their key direct report. Now you have two new layers to think about. If someone on your original list of regular contacts isn't really driving your company's future, one of the other two—one layer above and one layer below—almost certainly is. Now think ahead five years. How many of those people on your current list will be critical to your company's future five years from now? More important, think about who is not on that list who will be important in driving your company; that is, future drivers who aren't there now. Now you have a list of some of the key drivers who should be among your sources for gaining firsthand information.

Once you have identified who's driving your company, both now and in the future, you can do what Mike Ruettgers did routinely: Improve the quality of your time with those people by thinking more in advance about how you can transform what seem to be routine encounters into opportunities to probe and ask questions that you haven't asked before. Your contacts can provide you with new perspectives or firsthand information about your products and how they're used.

Rule#4: Empathy Is Essential

We know that there are biases and assumptions that color the information we get from filtered sources. But what about our own biases and assumptions? People hear what they want to hear, not necessarily what is being said. It's important in reaching the right decision that we put ourselves in the position of the source and try to understand what the source is saying from the source's perspective.

Think about Orin Smith. Here was a high-paid and powerful executive living in Seattle, one of the nation's great cities. Yet he was able, in part because of his small-town origins, to put himself in the shoes of residents of small towns and see how powerful their desire was to have a Starbucks where they lived. Mike Ruettgers put himself in the shoes of a harried CIO and thought about what that person needed to get things done more efficiently and effectively. It's called empathy, defined as a feeling of concern and understanding for another's situation and feelings, and it's essential to decision making. In fact, it's at the heart of some of the most consequential decisions that associate Supreme Court justice Stephen Breyer makes. His reasoning in the case of a seventeen-year-old boy illustrates how he applies the skill of putting himself in someone else's shoes.

The U.S. Supreme Court decides the most important and vexing cases that arise in our country. If they weren't so difficult to solve, they wouldn't make it all the way to the high court. Justice Breyer takes his job seriously and brings such intensity to his decisions that he needs several days of rest at the end of a Supreme Court session just to clear his head. When writing an opinion, he normally has to begin twice from scratch, revising as he goes along. Consider one example: *Yarborough v. Alvarado*.

Yarborough v. Alvarado involved a murder and a seventeen-year-old boy. The boy was brought to a police station, put in a room, and questioned by the police about a homicide. After two hours of questioning, the boy confessed to being involved in the murder. He was not, however, given the standard Miranda warning before the police began questioning him. A Miranda warning is what Hollywood is referring to when an officer barks out "Read him his rights." You've probably heard the police on *Law & Order* recite the warning: "You have the right to remain silent . . ." By law, the police must read someone the Miranda warning if that person is not free to leave, such as when a suspect is arrested.

The rule is that when you're in confinement, if you think you're not free to leave, then the police have to give you a Miranda warning. But if you're free to leave, then they don't. In this case, they didn't give the boy a Miranda warning, and he was later convicted of murder.

The case before the Court was about the boy's rights, not about whether he was involved in a murder. The question: Should he have been entitled to a Miranda warning?

The outcome of the Supreme Court vote was five to four against the boy. The Court concluded that since the boy was free to leave at any time, he was not entitled to a Miranda warning, and thus his rights were not violated.

But Justice Breyer's dissent makes clear that he thought there was a more basic question at the heart of the case: Did he reasonably think he was free to leave? The key question was not what he personally happened to think, but what would a reasonable person in this situation think?

So Justice Breyer put himself in the shoes of a seventeen-year-old boy thrown into questioning at a police station. Would a boy that age understand that he could leave freely at any time? Breyer's dissent—which required many revisions—tries to convey to the reader what it would be like to be that seventeen-year-old boy.

From the dissent:

> Alvarado hears from his parents that he is needed for police questioning. His parents take him to the station. On arrival, a police officer separates him from his parents. His parents ask to come along, but the officer says they may not . . . Another officer says, "What do we have here; we are going to question a suspect." . . .
>
> The police take Alvarado to a small interrogation room, away from the station's public area. A single officer begins to question him, making clear in the process that the police have evidence that he participated in an attempted carjacking connected with a murder. When he says that he never saw any shooting, the officer suggests that he is lying, while adding that she is "giving [him] the opportunity to tell the truth" and "tak[e] care of [him]self.". . . Toward the end of the questioning, the officer gives him permission to take a bathroom or water break. After two hours, by which time he has admitted he was involved in the attempted theft, knew about the gun, and helped to hide it, the questioning ends.
>
> What reasonable person in the circumstances—brought to a police station by his parents at police request, put in a small interrogation room, questioned for a solid two hours, and confronted with claims that there is strong evidence that he participated in a serious crime—could have thought to himself, "Well, anytime I want to leave I can just get up and walk out"? If the person harbored any doubts, would he still think he might be free to leave once he recalls that the police officer has just refused to let his parents remain with him during questioning? Would he still think that he, rather than the officer, controls the situation?[8]

Breyer was putting himself in the boy's shoes, trying to understand what it was like to be a seventeen-year-old boy being questioned by the police in a small interrogation room. Breyer was asking, "What would a reasonable *seventeen-year-old person* in this situation think?" instead of "What would a reasonable person in this situation think?" He wanted his readers to put themselves in the same position and to understand that a seventeen-year-old might think differently.

Justice Breyer's dissent also makes clear that he thought there could be other, similar circumstances involved. Suppose that he was Hispanic, spoke little English, the police didn't speak Spanish, and there was no translator. Breyer's message: Put yourself in their position.

Whether you agree with Justice Breyer's opinion in this case, his empathy highlights a critical element of processing information from the source. Isn't putting yourself in the boy's shoes, fact by fact, the best way to assess what he would reasonably think? Whether you are reviewing case facts like Justice Stephen Breyer, meeting with customers like Mike Ruettgers, or observing doctors like Bill George, you must try to interpret the source from its perspective to avoid adding your own biases.

CHAPTER 2

Fill a Room with Barbarians

How would you like to work for a boss who requires you and your colleagues to sit in a tiny conference room arguing with one another for hours every time he had to make a tough decision?

Most of us try to avoid conflict. Yet conflict is exactly what Dean Kamen, founder of DEKA Research & Development Corporation, seeks and encourages. Kamen, whose company focuses on such radical new technologies as delivering chemotherapy to infants and helping people with kidney failure live normal lives, finds that bringing together people with diverse backgrounds and well-informed opinions to vehemently argue their positions helps him make his toughest decisions.

"I like it when ten people walk into the room with ten different opinions and are so passionate they're yelling at each other," says Kamen. Yet he admits that if someone from outside attended one of those meetings "they'd think we're all barbarians."

Not all decisions require extensive or full-throated argument. But when the choice is tough and there is no clear path forward, a hearty debate can be the best tool you have for uncovering the right solution. We aren't talking about seeking compromise. Tough decisions by their nature brook no compromise. Otherwise, they wouldn't be tough. To get the best thinking from their teams, wise leaders actively seek dissent.

Seeking and fostering dissent provides two advantages. First, it forces the participants to expose their opinions to a wide range of counterarguments. The strengths and weaknesses of each opinion surface for all to see and think about as each viewpoint is tested against the strongest possible challenge. Second, diverse and well-founded arguments can reframe a problem so that everyone sees it in a new way. Suddenly, a unique solution can emerge that no one had considered before.

Yet argument alone can't solve problems. Wise leaders understand that as important as it is to bring into the open various points of view, it is equally important that the discussions take place in what we call a *culture of candor* in which employees are comfortable expressing their varied perspectives and just as comfortable working together to implement the resulting decision.

"I expect people to walk into the room carrying spears, ready to defend their position," says Kamen. "My job is to decide when we've had enough battle and make a decision. And when people leave the room, everybody's got to be working toward the same goal."

Vigorous debate can easily degenerate into chaos, an unfocused shout-fest that leaves participants angry, resentful, and unsatisfied and little or no progress made toward the decision. That's why creating the culture of candor is so important. Participants accept and embrace the highly charged atmosphere of the room. They know that when it is over, there will be no winners or losers, just honest opinions honestly rendered. People can say whatever they want as long as they avoid personal attacks. When a person presents an opinion—and everyone is expected to come prepared and to have an opinion—it is expected that others will challenge it. As the leader, you may facilitate the debate, but your opinions are no more valuable than and just as vulnerable to attack as anyone else's. Truth is the goal, and when the decision finally emerges, everyone is expected to sign on to support it.

An established culture of candor goes beyond just ensuring that the barbarians in the room walk out willing to move forward with the decision. It also makes people more lively and productive and inspires them to better personal relations with their peers. If the debates are done in the right atmosphere, people will look forward to the sessions. But most important of all, when a culture of candor is established, consensus is no longer needed to keep the peace. Leaders can make the *right* decisions rather than inferior and compromised decisions.

"OUR QUALITY STINKS!"

Bob Galvin was worried. Since succeeding his legendary father Paul as the CEO of Motorola, Galvin had spent twenty years building the company's reputation and profits. Outsiders saw an innovative company that had been at the forefront of electronic and communications technology, including pagers, two-way radios, and semiconductors. And during Galvin's tenure as CEO, sales had risen from $200 million to almost $3 billion. Yet, in 1979, Galvin knew that something was amiss.

"I had a sense that somehow we really weren't tackling all the problems we needed to tackle," says Galvin. Like other American manufacturing companies, Motorola was feeling increasing competitive pressure from Japan. Galvin felt Motorola was ripe for a big change. Without knowing what that change was, he issued a call to action to his top officers. He summoned all eighty-eight of the top managers from around the world to Motorola's first-ever company-wide officers' meeting, a three-day affair to be held at the Ambassador West Hotel in downtown Chicago. The mission: Map out new initiatives for Motorola's corporate renewal.

Many managers weren't happy about the idea. Motorola executives were productive, efficient, and frugal. Some of them, knowing that they could speak candidly to Galvin, grumbled to him about the expense, in both time and money, of spending three days in a Chicago hotel. Others hated the idea of a formal dinner Saturday night at which they would be required to wear tuxedos. But Galvin urged them to keep an open mind and to think about the future of their company. He had outlined an agenda that included broad topics such as "The Customer, Our Integrity, Our People" that were designed to inspire renewed confidence and a sense of purpose.[1] But he also set out some narrow topics about such things as how to better transfer information from engineering to the factories. He hoped the wide-ranging agenda would spark discussion that would show him how to set the company on a new path.

The meeting began on a Friday in April 1979 and opened with a speech by Carl Lindholm, a vice president, whose topic was "How to Get Along with the Chief Executive Office." The speech gently mocked the three-person office of the chief executive, which included Galvin, Bill Weisz, and John Mitchell, referring to them as "the Three Bears" and "the Holy Trinity." But it also contained some hard truths about how the three top executives didn't always listen carefully, weren't available when they were needed, and sometimes acted a little officious.

"It was the funniest damned speech and he got a lot of laughs," Galvin says. "But he also found some faults and he called us on them and we said, 'Fine, we'll have to fix that.' It gave the meeting substance because people were talking the truth, the reality that we all have to figure out a way to do things better."

By Saturday afternoon, most of the executives were thoroughly engaged in a wide-ranging discussion about reviving their company. Then, in a short question-and-answer session before a scheduled refreshment break, Art Sundry stood up. Art was a respected figure among the Motorola executives. As the national sales manager of two-way radios, he was running Motorola's most profitable business with an astounding 85 percent global market share. Everyone turned their attention to what he would say.

"We aren't talking about the most important subject, and I'm afraid we're going to go through the entire meeting and never talk about it," he said. "The subject we ought to be talking about is that our quality stinks!"

It took a moment for that statement to sink in among the executives. Motorola was a revered company, a household name. Its quality assurance programs had produced some significant advances. Yet here was the guy running the most successful business, and he was saying the company's quality stinks?

"Art pretty much put the kibosh on anything else in the question-and-answer period," Galvin says. "So we go for our refreshment break and everybody was talking. They were saying things like 'Wow, that was a powerful statement' and 'You know what? He's right' and 'I thought my quality was pretty good. Maybe Art's seeing something I'm not.' "

The entire focus of the meeting suddenly changed. Quality became the first and foremost issue on the table. Each executive did some soul-searching and most could confess that the quality in their business unit wasn't as good as it should be. At that night's formal dinner, all the conversations were about quality. The executives were so involved in the discussion about quality that they didn't even complain about having to wear tuxedos.

By the end of the weekend session, Galvin and the officers decided to focus on product quality as the best way to reinvigorate Motorola. They reached that conclusion only after one of their colleagues had spoken his mind without fear of retribution or ridicule. It was part of the culture of candor that Bob Galvin had cultivated for years, a lesson he had learned from his father and one that had benefited him when he was a young executive with no engineering background, dependent upon the people under him for guidance.

"It was well known in the organization that you could speak up in my presence," he says. "Our people knew they could say anything in front of me. I don't think that in other companies Sundry would have had the courage to stand up in front of so many people and say the company's quality stinks, but he knew he could do that at Motorola. We had created an atmosphere in which people could speak and influence the company."

Sundry's statement touched a nerve among his colleagues because they recognized the truth of his harsh remark. Sundry himself brought the subject to their attention because he was getting complaints from police departments, truckers, and taxicab drivers that used Motorola's two-way radios. And that was just in his business unit. Any one of the eighty-eight executives could have pointed to other evidence that had been mounting for some time.

They all knew, for example, what had happened to Motorola's television business. From their inception, television sets had been manufactured using vacuum tubes, which along with other components were prone to frequent failure, a trend that gave rise to a fast-growing profession: television repairman. Eventually, the invention of transistors allowed electronics manufacturers not only to get rid of the tubes, but also to use much-smaller solid-state-circuit modules within a television set. Motorola was in the forefront of that trend. In 1967, the company introduced its solid-state Quasar model, which boasted of its "works in a drawer." A repairman could easily unplug and replace a failed circuit in the field rather than hauling the television off to his shop.

Japanese electronics manufacturers took another route. As Japan rebuilt its industrial base after World War II, many industries, including the automotive and electronics industries, were eager to free themselves from their reputations for cheap, flimsy products. To do that, they paid close attention to the teachings of people such as Joe Juran and W. Edwards Deming, American engineers and statistical analysts who preached a gospel of careful quality control that ensured a product was made right the first time. In their philosophy, there was no room for field failures. While Motorola was pioneering better ways to fix television sets, Japanese manufacturers were making television sets that didn't need to be fixed.

The result was a humbling erosion of market share for Motorola. Galvin and his colleagues saw the trend going decisively to the Japanese and sold Motorola's television operations to Matsushita in 1974. Then came another humiliation when Matsushita, manufacturing television sets in a former Motorola factory and using the same equipment and some of the same workers, began churning out television sets with one-twentieth the failure rates of the Motorola sets that had been built there.[2]

Quality had been a part of Motorola's ethos for years. But it was focused mostly on service to customers, not engineering and manufacturing. After the Chicago meeting, Galvin himself set out to see how bad Motorola's quality was by visiting many of the company's customers. "I did not want to see any big shots," he recalls. "I wanted to see the people who installed, who serviced, who wrote the checks to us, who received the material, who assembled it into their products, the purchasing people and so on."

The results were sobering. After just four visits, he could predict what he would hear from customers: "We like doing business with you. But we would do 10, or 20, or 30 percent—maybe even 300 percent—more business with you if you would just stop making so many mistakes." The mistakes they cited ranged from incorrect invoices that had to be corrected to DOA (dead-on-arrival) radios.

"We had become too tolerant of errors because we were doing better than GE, better than RCA, better than all the others in our business," Galvin says. "If we shipped fifty radios to a police department and two of them didn't work, we'd say 'Gee, 4 percent of them didn't work. If I got a 96 percent from my teacher in school, that was pretty good.' The thing that was so bad about the quality was that the customer didn't like it. If we made a mistake, the customer was inconvenienced and had to do something two or three times to get it right. Art didn't have to draw us a picture, he just awakened us because his was the best of our businesses, and it was imperfect."

But recognizing that quality was a problem and doing something about it were two different problems. After the Chicago weekend meeting, Motorola's executives were taking the quality problem seriously, but without achieving much.

"Monday morning, people returned to their offices and started to work on quality control," recalls Galvin. "They didn't know what formally they were supposed to do, but they did a little bit here and a little bit there."

"A little bit here, a little bit there" clearly wasn't going to solve Motorola's quality problems, and Galvin decided to push harder.

"I became impatient with the fact that my senior associates, who were doing a remarkable job as general managers, were focused all too much on budgets and forecasts and things like that.

Those are essential, but quality wasn't being given the same amount of attention, and I finally lost patience with that fact. Quality deserved equal status. So I proclaimed that from that point forward quality would be the first subject on every agenda from the board meeting to every other meeting in the company."

Then came the big break. A meticulous engineer and quality assurance executive took advantage of Galvin's culture of candor. Bill Smith called the CEO to tell him that he may have found the answer to Motorola's quest for quality.

"I knew Bill Smith was a top engineer in our communications business, though I did not know Bill very well," Galvin says. "He said, 'Bob, I have got an important idea and concept I have got to express to you, and I think it is very important to the company. I would like to see you.'"

Galvin quickly set aside time to meet with Smith. The engineer laid out for Galvin a sophisticated theory of how latent defects in industrial processes and products create failures and customer dissatisfaction. "I have to admit I did not understand what Bill was talking about," Galvin recalls. But he adds, "I was sure as the devil I understood that *he* knew what he was talking about."

Galvin invited Smith back the next day to explain it all again and began to understand the implications of Smith's ideas for improving quality. Then he sent Smith to see two senior executives with engineering backgrounds. They understood almost immediately what he was talking about and enthusiastically began to figure out how to put Smith's concepts to work.

While based on statistical quality control ideas that had been developed and implemented by people like Juran and Deming,

Smith's unique approach to using those ideas became what is known today as Six Sigma, a Motorola trademark and the most widely utilized quality control process in the world. When Bob Galvin retired as Motorola's chairman in 1990, Six Sigma was saving the company $700 million a year and Motorola was competing head-to-head with the Japanese electronics titans.[3] It all started with a culture of candor that let people like Art Sundry speak their mind without fear of reprisal or recrimination.

BETTER OR BEST?

The room was packed. Some of the more than twenty engineers jammed into the conference room were standing or leaning against the exposed brick walls. And the voices were rising. It was time to make a decision, and each of the two teams clamored to make their points. The engineers who had been working on the three-wheel cluster for months had some powerful arguments. The design was already far along. They had a prototype that used three-wheel clusters. The sponsor had seen it and liked it.

But the engineers who had been struggling to work out the kinks in a two-wheel cluster argued that their approach had inherent advantages. The wheels could be bigger so they could climb curbs. More important, the two-wheel cluster allowed the chair to fit under a dining room table or an office desk.

"Maybe," said a challenger, "but that's assuming you can make it work with two-wheel clusters, and I don't think you can."

When your company is designing the world's most advanced motorized wheelchair and tapping the imaginations and analytical abilities of world-class engineers to do it, you're going to get some arguments. And that's exactly what Dean Kamen wanted. Arguments. Lots of them. And he liked them loud. He was counting on the arguments to pave the way to the best solution for handicapped people.

Kamen is one of the world's most prolific inventors. The inventions that emerge from DEKA Research & Development Corporation, his research lab in New Hampshire, are on the cutting edge of technological innovation and can cost tens of millions of dollars to develop. This project, the iBOT, promised an incredible range of mobility to the disabled. The guiding principle behind the design was to mimic human balance. Not only would the wheelchair rise and balance itself so that the occupant would be at eye level with people who were standing, it would also climb stairs. Its multiwheel drive system could traverse rough terrain and ride over barriers such as curbs.

DEKA partnered with Johnson & Johnson to develop the new chair. The original concept called for two four-wheel clusters, one on each side of the chair. That idea was quickly scrapped in favor of simpler and more compact three-wheel clusters. Now the engineers who had been developing the chair felt they had solved most of the biggest problems. They had designed, tested, and redesigned one component after another, logging thousands of hours of "seat time" in the chair, testing it with stairs, ramps, and high grocery shelves. They even had an automobile in the lab to work out the easiest way to move from the chair to a car. To accomplish all this, they had devised a complex system of gyroscopes, motors, fast-feedback control circuits, and software that would give the chair its amazing capabilities. The engineers were proud of their work and eager to move from development to production in concert with J&J.

But Kamen had long been pondering a larger question: Was the three-wheel cluster the *best* solution for the people who would be using the chair? Wouldn't a two-wheel cluster be much better? Several months earlier, he had funded a small "skunk works" effort separate from the iBOT design team to test the concept of two-wheel clusters. The engineers working on that project had made considerable progress and learned a lot. They knew that the two-wheel clusters would clearly be better for wheelchair users. The seat of the chair could be lower so that the occupant could pick up a pencil off the floor or roll up to a dining table. Yet when the chair was elevated, it would be taller, so that the occupant would be at eye level with people standing nearby. But they also knew they confronted some real challenges. A chair with two-wheel clusters would need considerably more sophisticated balancing controls, much sturdier hardware, and a bigger motor and battery. Given enough time and money, they believed they could overcome those hurdles, but they couldn't guarantee it.

As the debate in the crowded conference room went on, the proponents of the two-wheel clusters convinced everyone that if they could solve the problems, a chair using the two-wheel clusters would be better. But they didn't convince the engineers pushing the three-wheel version that they could solve those problems. And even if they could, the three-wheel advocates noted, the two-wheel clusters couldn't climb stairs as smoothly as the three-wheel cluster design. More to the point, they knew how many millions of dollars had been spent getting to this stage. J&J had signed off on the three-wheel cluster design, and it was time to get moving.

"We're so far along now, the last thing we need now is a change," argued one engineer.

Kamen listened carefully as the increasingly heated arguments surged back and forth. This wasn't going like most decision-making meetings at DEKA. Usually, the debaters converged on a common solution. These guys were getting further and further apart!

"Most of the time when you find the decision getting harder and harder to make, it's because it sort of doesn't matter. By definition, if you're having a hard time deciding, it's because they're approximately equal," he says. "This time, the more we talked about it, the more it seemed that the two-wheel design would be way better than the three-wheel design. It also seemed that it would be way harder to do. We had people saying, 'I told you so, you can't possibly do this,' and the other half was saying, 'This is such an obvious win, we've got to make it work.' "

Finally, Kamen called a halt. "We're here to try to help a bunch of people with mobility issues, and if we can't make this thing fit under a desk or a table, then that will be a big loss," he told the engineers. Then he announced his decision: Rather than choose either design, he told the engineers he was going to fund parallel development tracks. If over a short period of time the proponents of the two-wheel clusters couldn't make the design work, then DEKA would complete the development of the chair using three-wheel clusters. If, on the other hand, the engineers could create the necessary software and controls to make the two-wheel chair work, that would be the chair that DEKA would produce.

"We're not going to finish both chairs," he told the engineers. "I know I'm pissing away money on one of them; I just don't know which one I'm pissing away the money on. You're going to come back here in a month, and you're either going to be more confident that a two-wheel cluster can do this job, or more confident that it's more trouble than we thought."

The decision would cost DEKA millions as both teams proceeded with their separate designs. But it made sense, he says. "It was the only rational thing to do, because the upside of the two-wheel cluster was so big, but the downside risk of it not working was equally big. The two-wheel design was a high-reward, high-risk option. By continuing with the three-wheel design, we basically eliminated the risk because we knew it would work."

It took longer than a month for the engineers who favored the two-wheel cluster to devise the software and controls that would make it work. But as soon as they proved their design to Kamen's satisfaction, he made the decision to go with the two-wheel cluster.

"We had a lot of big fights, literally fights, not people against people, but fights that pitted one technology against another and different ideas about systems," Kamen says. "I finally told them that I've heard all the arguments and I'm glad we had them, and now everybody's got to get behind doing whatever it takes to make the two-wheel product. A lot of people were not enthusiastic about it at the time, but I think everybody now believes it was the right decision."

Filling a room full of barbarians to debate different approaches to solving a problem can change your perspective and lead you in a new direction. The argument over the best design for the iBOT wheelchair is nothing out of the ordinary for DEKA. Arguments like the one over iBOT design inform everything the company does, and Kamen looks specifically for people who can engage in heated arguments and emerge from the room with their confidence intact regardless of whether their arguments prevail.

"I tell them, 'Bring your best opinion to the meeting and don't be intimidated by me or anybody else. Stand behind it, yell, scream, attack other ideas with a vengeance, do whatever you want as long as you don't attack other people.' We want to get the best ideas, and we want to attack the bad ideas with as much force as we can and let the Darwinian system weed them out."

Kamen's approach—using debate to flush out the issues that guide him to a decision—relies on a culture of candor carried to the extreme. Few wise leaders encourage their subordinates to yell and scream, yet seeking dissent is a hallmark of their decision-making process. Each of them brings together a diverse collection of people armed with ideas and ready to do battle over the solutions to problems. But they leave the conference room ready to execute whatever decision their debate has produced.

"THIS IS SOMETHING WE HAVE TO DO"

Time was of the essence. Mexico had billions of dollars in short-term debt coming due within weeks and no money to make the payments. Private lenders had all but stopped lending to the government. Default loomed. If Mexico defaulted, the ripple effects—reduced international trade, disruption to financial markets, internal strife, and a massive influx of illegal immigrants— would damage the U.S. economy. The president of the United States turned to his top economic advisers for advice.

Larry Summers, the top Treasury Department official for international affairs, and his boss, Robert Rubin, began huddling in a Treasury Department conference room, sometimes joined by Federal Reserve chairman Alan Greenspan, to thrash out a recommendation. In what amounted to a rolling meeting that went on for eight to ten hours each day, the advisers and their subordinates worked through one issue after another. What were the risks? Could those risks be mitigated and, if so, how? What were the consequences of not acting?

Some of the risks were obvious. Mexico simply might be unable to repay any loans, and the money lent to the government would be lost. Others weren't so apparent. Investors earlier had been buying Mexico's high-yielding bonds with little or no regard to the risk implied by those high rates. If Mexico defaulted, those investors would lose hundreds of millions of dollars. But if the United States rescued Mexico, the bondholders would continue to receive their big payouts and, worse, might be tempted to speculate on other risky debt in the expectation of being bailed out.

The three advisers decided early in the process that the United States should try to rescue Mexico, but only under certain conditions. The United States, they decided, should put pressure on the Mexican government to establish and follow policies designed to put its economy on a sound footing. They also wanted to reassure investors that lending to Mexico in the future would not be as risky. Finally, they wanted to preserve U.S. credibility. If whatever rescue package the United States fashioned didn't work, the rest of the world would question our intentions and ability. Any single one of those objectives would be difficult enough, but to satisfy all three required tough deliberation.

The questions kept mounting even as the clock was winding down. Should any loans be given in tranches so that the United States could minimize its losses in case the rescue began to look as if it were failing? And what about collateral for the loans? One idea was to use Mexico's oil production as collateral. If the loans didn't work and Mexico defaulted, the United States could be repaid with oil. But then someone pointed out that if Mexico defaulted, there would be chaos in the country, with people flowing over the borders and others going hungry, hardly auspicious conditions to be diverting much-needed money from Mexico's oil sales to the U.S. Treasury.

When the details of a recommended package finally emerged, Rubin and Summers briefed President Bill Clinton. They laid out the mechanics of the plan, but then they also laid out all the risks and their explanations for why they thought the risks were acceptable. Clinton readily accepted both the recommendations and the risks.

"This is what the American people sent us here to do," he said.[4]

Then disaster struck. Congress rejected the package, with each party expressing different reasons. "The Republicans didn't see why we should bail out a country that did active diplomacy with Castro," recalls Summers, "and the Democrats didn't see why we should bail out a country that was not giving full labor rights to the Zapatistas. And then there were people who didn't see why we should fund a country that wasn't doing enough to control immigration."

Now what? There was little time left, and it seemed that Clinton's commitment to saving Mexico would fail. The politics were also getting more troublesome. A poll published in the *Los Angeles Times* showed that 79 percent of the American public was opposed to a rescue effort.[5] But there was still one possibility: the Exchange Stabilization Fund. Congress had created the ESF in 1934 when the United States went off the gold standard as a tool for the Treasury Department to stabilize exchange rates. No one then could have foreseen the threat that a default by a developing country could pose to the United States. But Summers and Rubin believed President Clinton could use the $35 billion in the ESF without Congress's approval, although they also warned that he could only do it once.[6] Congress would almost certainly place limits on the ESF if Clinton defied its will.

Again Clinton didn't hesitate. "Look, this is something we have to do," he told Rubin and Summers.[7]

Mexico received a $40 billion aid package, half of which came from the United States, while the other half was provided by the International Monetary Fund and Canada. The rescue was successful. The aid package gave Mexico the breathing room it needed to turn around the country's financial situation. Mexico didn't even need the full amount and repaid the bailout loans ahead of schedule.[8]

Summers believes that those tense few weeks in January 1995 ended well for two reasons. First, a culture of candor enveloped the debate about whether and what kind of rescue package to offer Mexico. That vigorous debate identified and analyzed all the risks associated with a rescue effort for Mexico.

"We laid out the risks along with our recommendation, and I think the president was much more comfortable accepting our recommendation because he knew we had thought very hard about the risks," he explains. Had Rubin and Summers not candidly explained the risks to President Clinton, he might have been much less comfortable making his decision in the face of huge uncertainty.

Second, Clinton's decision was the result of top advisers testing their ideas against the strongest possible challenge. Such tests have always been a cornerstone of Summers's decision making, whether in his position as an economics professor at Harvard, as undersecretary and later secretary of the U.S. Treasury, or as president of Harvard.

"If I've got to make a policy decision, I don't want anyone to be able to come up to me after I've made that decision and make a criticism of it that I haven't already thought of," Summers says. "That means I haven't thought about it enough and I've done my job badly. I'm not comfortable doing anything unless I see very clearly both sides of what a decision may mean. If the people I'm looking to for advice have already developed a complete set of downsides and they've clearly thought about them and I've had a chance to think about them, then I'll be comfortable with the decision. But if somebody just says, 'I think we ought to do X,' then I'm likely to say, 'What are the best three reasons for not doing X?' "

But examining every angle of a question or idea *without* a culture of candor can be disastrous, as Summers himself discovered. In January 2005, Summers attempted to spark a debate when he

was a featured speaker at a National Bureau of Economic Research conference. As an economist and the president of Harvard, Summers was asked to discuss and to engage the audience
on why so few women hold tenured appointments in math and
science at major universities. The idea of fostering such a debate
appealed to Summers's keen interest in examining big questions.
But Summers inadvertently overstepped the bounds when, quot-
ing research, he seemed to be suggesting that natural predilec-
tions might help explain the lack of tenured women. His
comments, misinterpreted, touched off not a debate, but a furor
that brought opprobrium on him from every corner. He apolo-
gized more than once but to no avail. In June 2006, he resigned as
president of Harvard to quell the discord that had arisen among
faculty members over his remarks. In retrospect, Summers ac-
knowledges that he should have first tested his controversial remarks with people close to him who would tell him candidly if
they thought he was going too far and inviting attack. While he
idealistically believed that an academic seminar was a suitable
place to exchange ideas, he found belatedly that it was not a place
that shared a culture of candor.

Difficult decisions are often difficult because they will have
profound consequences. That's why it is so important that the
ideas that will form the foundation of a difficult decision are
thoroughly analyzed and tested through rigorous challenges.
Not only does the back-and-forth of serious debate result in the
best ideas coming to the top, it also identifies the potential problems and hurdles that may arise when executing the decision.
The knowledge that the pros as well as the cons of a decision

have been argued and refined provides a level of confidence that is lacking in snap decisions or decisions made "from the gut."

RULES FOR DEVELOPING A CULTURE OF CANDOR

Filling a room with barbarians who can willingly engage in vociferous argument yet be able to walk out of the conference room united isn't easy. It requires a careful balance of the right people in the right environment. It goes without saying that the participants have to have good ideas grounded in reality and backed with solid reasoning. But not only must they be able to articulate those ideas and defend them against the strongest challenges, they also have to be willing to attack ideas offered by others. A room full of barbarians isn't a place for shy, retiring types. A culture of candor is absolutely essential to bringing out the best from barbarians. They have to know they can speak without fear of punishment or retribution, and they have to be willing to accept the decision that emerges from debate and work together to execute it.

Rule #1: Require Full Participation

When you fill a room with barbarians to argue the various merits of different solutions to a problem, you need every point of view and idea that you can muster. That means everyone must participate. There is no room for idlers or observers.

The principle that everyone needs to make his or her own

views known pervades the institution that makes some of the nation's most crucial decisions: the U.S. Supreme Court. After the justices have read the briefs, heard the oral arguments, and had time to reflect on the case, the group convenes in a conference room with no one else present. They then go around the table, one by one, expressing their views of the case. The chief justice leads off, followed by the remaining eight justices in order of seniority. Justice Breyer explains how the process works: "The rule is that no one speaks twice until everybody has spoken once. It's absolutely enforced. No matter how great an idea you have in the middle, nobody speaks out of turn. Everybody speaks once and then we go back. It's a very, very helpful rule."

Of course, Supreme Court judges have no fear about expressing their opinions. But that isn't always true in corporate conference rooms. That's why it is so important to create a culture of candor that demands people speak out. Bob Galvin recalls a meeting during his tenure at Motorola that brought together a handful of senior executives to try to solve a vexing problem in one of the company's factories. After lengthy discussion, Galvin thought it was time to put the group on the path to making a decision. He went around the table asking each executive his opinion.

"We got around to John, who was the comptroller. Neat guy. He knew the numbers backward and forward. I said, 'John, what do you think?' And he replied, 'Well, I don't think I should have a recommendation. I'm in the role of providing all the facts, and I think I've given everybody all the facts they need.' "

The round-the-table polling continued until everyone had offered a view. A decision was made and announced and the meeting adjourned. "As everybody started to leave my little office, I asked John to hang back," Galvin says. "After he had closed the door, I said, 'Don't ever do that again. Don't ever fail to take advantage of making a recommendation. A recommendation is the seed of a decision that will be made. The next time anybody asks you for your recommendation, have one. You're the best in your field, and it will be a good recommendation.' And after that John had a recommendation every time anyone asked."

Rule #2: Forbid Carryover

The toughest decisions are made one at a time. There will be winners and losers each time, but they're seldom the same for each decision. And there's no room for trade-offs or back scratching when it comes to these decisions. That's why it's important to follow the Supreme Court's lead and enforce the "no carryover rule." Justice Breyer explains how the rule works: "There is no carryover from one case to another. There is absolutely none of this 'you vote this way in this case and I'll vote that way on the next one.' Absolutely zero. A coalition exists only for that one case. The next case may result in a different coalition. People will tend to decide similar cases in similar ways, of course, but there's no bargaining, not even implicitly."

Very few Supreme Court decisions result in a 9–0 vote. The no carryover rule ensures that the justices walk out of the conference room with closure after each case is decided. It allows each new discussion to start with a clean slate. They are free to say what they wish because they know it will not be held against them during future decisions. They act in a culture of candor.

"Tomorrow is another day," says Justice Breyer, "and you start it fresh. There's no carryover, and that makes for very good personal relations. The case is over, fine, it's on to the next one."

Getting advice from a room full of barbarians requires that they make independent judgments. By that we mean their opinions are independently developed and that each time they participate in a decision-making debate they have no reason to compromise to support someone else's opinion. If, over the course of time, you begin to see the same coalition forming each time, take a closer look. It may be nothing more than coincidence, but it might also be a symptom that someone is violating the no-carryover rule.

Rule #3: Seek Diversity of Opinions

Effective debate starts before the team walks in the room. The selection of who will participate determines how effective the debate will be. A debate among people with a diverse array of experiences, expertise, and perspectives creates the best environment for debate. When Bob Galvin sought out the perspective of all Motorola's senior officers, he wanted a fresh way of looking at the problems facing the company. Having people with differing responsibilities helps in developing new alternatives, like Art Sundry's suggestion to focus on quality. After all, your decision can only be as good as your best alternative. Getting marketing, operations, sales, and research all talking together ensures that the best alternatives get brought forward.

Dean Kamen wants to see his room of barbarians filled with

employees who have different ways of thinking about the same problem. "If I have ten people in the room, and I think they're all smart and I'm paying them all for all the passion they have on this subject, if I don't get ten violently supported different opinions, there are some people in that room who are wasting oxygen."

When people are engaged in debate, the collective wisdom of a diverse group not only creates alternatives, it also fleshes out the nuances of the alternatives being discussed. The point is to ensure that the decision maker himself hears all the relevant nuances. That's why Justice Breyer looks for clerks who are not only extremely talented, but who will also challenge his positions on decisions.

"I prefer it when they have different positions," he says. "I want clerks who will produce different arguments. I want to be sure that they act as sounding boards, that they will think of things that are wrong. Being helpful means if I'm saying something wrong, don't let me say it."

When you're assembling a group of people to generate a discussion aimed at reaching an important decision, think carefully about the participants. They need to know enough about the nature of the decision you're trying to make that they will have a well-informed opinion and be prepared to state it and defend it. But they needn't be part of the group working on solving the problem. At DEKA, Dean Kamen usually includes engineers working on other projects in the discussions leading up a tough decision. He often finds that the "outsiders" can bring a fresh approach to a problem.

Over time, it will become clear who is worth inviting to these

sessions and who should be excluded. Someone chronically unprepared for the discussion or whose ego is easily bruised by the
give-and-take of debate need not be invited back. And while the
discussion is happening, don't hesitate to enforce the rule that attacks can be made against ideas, but never against people.

Further, a diverse team can also challenge one another by
purposefully taking on different roles. Kleiner Perkins Caufield
& Byers, one of Silicon Valley's most successful venture capital
firms, utilizes this principle of diversity when it makes its investment decisions. Like most venture capital firms, Kleiner Perkins
is a partnership—each partner owns a piece of its fund's ultimate
performance. Nearly all of the partners' compensation comes
from this performance.

Before Kleiner Perkins decides to invest in a new company,
the partners must all agree. Will Hearst, a partner in the firm,
likens the atmosphere to one of a diverse family. "If one person's
the athlete, someone else has to be the student, and somebody
else has to be the artist," says Hearst. When the partnership sits
in a room to decide on an investment, each partner has a question he focuses in on. For one it is "Do we have the right CEO?"
For another it is "What's the big breakthrough here?" And for a
third it is "Why is everything going to go well?" As Hearst sum-
marizes, "That's the real benefit of the partnership process, this
multibinocular vision."

Rule #4: Quash the Pocket Veto

Even in a culture of candor, people can still stymie implementation simply by putting their hands in their pockets, quietly refus-

ing to execute a decision. Wise leaders prize employees who persuasively argue their opinions before a decision is made, yet who can abandon internal politics and come together as a team to implement the final choice. An essential task in achieving this is to eliminate the "pocket veto."

The term *pocket veto* comes from politics, where a pocket veto is the indirect rejection of a bill by the president of the United States. The U.S. Constitution gives the president ten days (excluding Sundays) to review and sign a piece of legislation once Congress has passed it. If the president chooses not to sign the bill into law within those ten days, and Congress adjourns during that time, the bill automatically dies.

The pocket veto can be an equally powerful tool in business. A member of your team can hear your final decision and then quietly undermine it through inaction. Mike Ruettgers ran into that problem when he was CEO of EMC.

"For a while we had a problem with pocket vetoes," he recalls. "I would make a decision and announce it and a few of the participants would walk out saying to themselves, 'I don't care what Mike thinks, I'm not doing that.' "

But Ruettgers found a solution. After he announced a decision, he would go around the room asking each person individually if they intended to pocket veto his decision.

"We would essentially ratify the decision by going around the room and asking, 'Are you comfortable with this? Okay.' In many cases, because you know from past experience that some of these people are pocket vetoers, you might ask them directly, 'I'm not going to see a pocket veto on this, am I, from you?' Then they finally have to say, 'Yes, I'll go along with it.' And once they do that, it becomes pretty much impossible for them to go and do it after they committed not to do it. The consequences of saying one thing in the meeting and then going and doing something different would be bad."

Mike Ruettgers knew who the pocket vetoers were in his organization and found a way to co-opt them into supporting his decision even if they didn't like it. He knew the power of a spoken commitment—"Yes, I'll go along with it"—effectively quashed the pocket veto. You may find that as you build your room of barbarians, you won't need to explicitly demand a commitment. Dean Kamen expects his barbarians to buckle down and execute whatever decision is made regardless of which side of the debate they were on. But if you find your decisions being sandbagged and you want to keep a talented pocket vetoer aboard, try getting individual spoken commitments to support your decision. That might just be all you'll need to do.

CHAPTER 3

Conquer the Fear of Risk

Got a coin handy? Here's a proposition. Flip it. If it comes up heads, we'll send you $1,000. If it comes up tails, you write us a check for $500. Would you be willing to take that gamble?

Probably not.

Princeton psychologist Daniel Kahneman often poses questions like this, and most people turn down the gamble despite the fact the odds are stacked in their favor.

"People really don't like that gamble because they might lose," Kahneman says. "Our brains are programmed to worry substantially about the possibility of loss, and not enough about the size of the loss relative to the gain. We don't like to lose, period."

Kahneman calls this penchant "loss aversion." It's a powerful psychological urge that causes people to put far greater weight on losing than on winning. Kahneman's studies reveal that people experience the pain of loss nearly twice as strongly as they enjoy gains of the same magnitude.[1]

Steering clear of gambles on the flip of a coin is one thing. But the propensity to avoid loss can be a big problem for business.

Business leaders can get so caught up in the possibility of losing that they ignore the realities of a situation. The fear of loss clouds their thinking, and they wind up shying away from taking a risk even when the probability of winning big is high.

Loss aversion is endemic at every level of most companies. People fear to take risks because they believe a bad outcome will hurt their chances for promotion and higher pay. The result is that entire organizations spend vast amounts of time, energy, and money seeking the safest options rather than those that offer the greatest risk-adjusted returns.

"If they feel they'll get fired if they lose or other bad things will happen to them, it's natural for employees to be more risk-averse than the higher-ups would like them to be," explains Kahneman, who won the Nobel Prize in 2002 for his pioneering work in behavioral economics. "How to promote more risk taking in an organization is a formidable problem."

What if you could routinely overcome loss aversion? Think of the possibilities if your competitors, shrinking before the prospect of a possible loss, shun a move that you know has a very good possibility of succeeding. What a competitive advantage! Wise leaders are constantly searching for ways to use that advantage. They look carefully at the same high-reward/high-risk opportunities that others, driven by their irrational concern about potential losses, dismiss. The wise leaders want to figure out if the *perceived* risk is actually far greater than the *real* risk.

Zeroing in on the major driver of the risk, they use targeted research from experts, experiments, and fundamental questioning that often turns conventional thinking on its head to calibrate the decision's downside. In the rare occasions on which they hit the jackpot, they are able to shift opportunities from the "Danger Zone" (the upper-right-hand corner in the diagram below) into the "Profit Zone" and generate huge gains. When they're in the Profit Zone, others might shake their head in bewilderment over how much risk they're taking, but they know that their decision is a "smart risk"—it really isn't very risky and holds the potential for great gains.

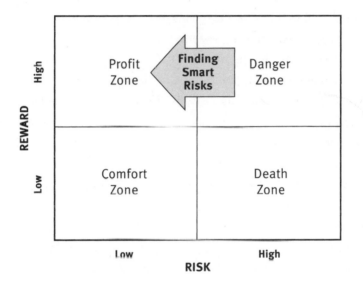

You can use the same approach that has worked so effectively for these wise leaders. But because the ideal low-risk and high-reward opportunities are relatively rare, you need to enlist your entire team as a force multiplier for finding those opportunities.

First, get their help in generating high-potential ideas on a regular basis. To do that, you have to create an atmosphere in which people believe they can propose high-potential ideas without being shot down or ridiculed.

Second, inspire your team members to do their own rational evaluation of their ideas. Depending on your operation and the incentives you can introduce, you can choose one of the variety of approaches that have worked so well for wise leaders: awarding bonuses for taking smart risks, extra time and funding for people to pursue their own ideas, uncapped upside potential, and, perhaps most important, a promotion system that rewards people for taking intelligent risks even when the outcomes aren't good.

Wise leaders and their teams conquer the fear of risk by using dispassionate analysis to discover the smart risks and profit tremendously. When they find the rare opportunity in the Profit Zone, they seize it. If the wise leaders in this chapter had shunned risk, the world might not have portable kidney dialysis, Shelly Lazarus might not be one of the fifty most powerful women in business, and The Blackstone Group might not have reaped the huge gains in both profit and prestige that it has enjoyed.[2]

SHINING A LIGHT ON THE BOGEYMAN

Asbestos.

For centuries regarded as a miracle mineral, the very word today conjures up images of miners and industrial workers suffering from asbestosis, a scarring of the lungs that makes breathing difficult, or mesothelioma, the deadly cancer caused principally by inhalation of asbestos particles. Asbestos litigation involves hundreds of thousands of claims against thousands of companies and is the longest-running mass tort litigation in the history of the United States.[3]

Hardly surprising, then, that when some of the junior analysts at The Blackstone Group learned that a manufacturing company Blackstone was considering purchasing dealt with asbestos, they recommended rejecting the deal.

"The initial reaction of everyone was 'It's asbestos, keep away from it, it'll bankrupt the whole company,' " recalls Steve Schwarzman, who with Peter Peterson founded Blackstone in 1985 with $400,000 of their own money. Today, Blackstone is widely regarded as one of the most prescient, powerful, and successful private-equity firms in the world, managing over $100 billion in assets.[4]

Schwarzman thrives in the pressure-cooker environment that requires hundreds of significant decisions each year about which companies to buy, who will run them, how to finance them, and which ones to sell. But despite the pace of decisions, Schwarzman insists that each one be made only after thorough and rigorous analysis. That kind of analysis can require months of sixty- to eighty-hour weeks for the junior analysts working on the evaluation of a potential deal. Once asbestos had been identified in the manufacturing company, they felt it would be a waste of time to continue working on an evaluation that would surely come to naught. Certainly the competitors for the company thought so, too. Most of them disappeared when asbestos reared its ugly head.

But Schwarzman wasn't afraid of the asbestos bogeyman; he wanted to understand it. That his competitors were running away from the deal was just further motivation to learn precisely what the risk was. If Blackstone knew more about the asbestos risks than any competitor, it would be in a strong position to make a winning bid and generate huge profits from the acquisition. What he needed to know was whether the other firms' fears of asbestos were justified and if there were ways to mitigate the risk. He sent Blackstone's analysts back to the drawing board with a charge to become experts in all facets of asbestos. They were to seek out engineers, lawyers, physicians, and insurance experts to answer the myriad questions surrounding the potential deal. Schwarzman figured that the additional costs of doing all that research were relatively small in the overall scheme of the potential deal.

He was right. The detailed investigation of the asbestos risks turned up some surprising results. First, the asbestos was present only in a part that the manufacturing company purchased from a supplier. What's more, the asbestos was firmly sealed in that metal part, unable to escape into and contaminate the atmosphere. The danger to the manufacturer's employees and to the companies that bought the machinery was practically zero. But if some enterprising liability lawyer still tried to bring a case, that was okay, too, because research into asbestos litigation showed that the manufacturing company's insurance policies would cover any liabilities from past problems. The risk, if any, would be minimal.

"Even though some stripe-suited lawyers will sue anybody over asbestos, we looked at it as a business and, along with some legal advice, we said, 'You know what? Nobody's getting sick, we're taking asbestos sealed in a metal box that someone else manufactured and we're moving it from one place to another. It's crazy to think that's a big problem!' "

Blackstone went ahead with the purchase of the manufacturing company, and it turned out, as Schwarzman predicted, to be a lucrative investment.

Understanding risk, not fearing it, is a hallmark of Blackstone's approach to private-equity investing. The firm uses a simple set of principles that not only tells Blackstone executives what to do, but also what *not* to do to avoid undue risk, explains cofounder Pete Peterson. One principle is "adjacency." It dictates that the firm will avoid going into businesses that aren't built on a skill set the firm has. That principle permitted Blackstone to get into the real estate business, which requires the same kind of rigorous due diligence as the firm's original foray into private-equity investing, but kept Blackstone out of the underwriting business, where it had opportunities but no real expertise.

A second principle is "hiring the very, very best." It requires the company to focus not just on strategy, but also execution of the strategy. And execution, Peterson contends, begins with getting the best people. The search for that kind of executive talent delayed Blackstone's plans to get into new businesses such as restructuring and new regions such as India. But the delays to find the best talent are worth the price, Peterson says. "After you've had a few experiences with businesses run by people who aren't all that good and you have to live with the problems, you say to yourself, 'I don't need that anymore.' "

One important criterion for hiring the very best, Peterson says, is to find people who want to learn and understand rather than people who think they know what's right. He credits his wife with the description of people as either "porous" or "metallic."

"Metallic are people you know where inputs kind of bounce off of them because they know they're right," Peterson explains, "and porous people absorb and internalize."

Finally, Blackstone follows the principle of "only friendly situations." The premise is that the firm will not make investments in anything but a friendly situation in which it can help management and corporations solve their difficulties. That principle has put Blackstone in the forefront of an innovative kind of deal making called "corporative partnerships." When a corporation is eager to get into a new business for strategic reasons but doesn't have the funds, it can partner with Blackstone for a mutual gain. For example, Blackstone entered into a corporative partnership with Time Warner to buy Six Flags when it became available at a low price; Blackstone held the debt and gave Time Warner an option to buy the parks (and a major incentive to make them succeed) in the future. They have invested in thirty-five such companies, far more than any other firm.[5]

Schwarzman is adamant that while others may think Blackstone is taking big risks, he and his partners know they aren't. The company's approach to risk taking starts at the top, when the partners discuss how much overall risk the firm should take given the external environment. It doesn't happen often, Schwarzman says, but Blackstone will either reduce its risk profile in a shrinking economy or increase it in an expanding economy, often before competitors see what is happening.

"We'll be debating one deal or another and all the while I'm thinking about this, and when I think we're in a changing environment I'll say, 'We've got to change our attitude towards risk. We ought to be more aggressive, put more money out. It's going to look risky, but it isn't.' "

Yet even in that kind of culture, Schwarzman has to be on guard against loss aversion even among some of his senior associates. "Usually what happens is that the senior people are a little more negative than the junior people," he explains. "They worry too much. They want to engineer out all the risk. Part of my job is figuring out how much risk to let in. I have to say, 'Look, it's permitted to take a little more risk here, it's on the house account. Don't worry about it, but just know what we're doing.' "

Knowing what they're doing at Blackstone involves massive research, using any resource necessary to gain a deep understanding of potential risks. But it also involves figuring out where to focus and how to use the very targeted information that is developed.

"You have to be able to completely sort through the mountain of stuff and figure out what the two or three important things are and how they're going to come out," says Schwarzman. "You spend your time on the major drivers of success or failure, the things that are going to determine the outcomes."

Finally, Blackstone's continuing success is built on a culture of questioning. "Asking questions of others is not only an acceptable thing to do, but a desired thing," says Schwarzman. "From the lowest person to the highest person in the organization, everyone has the right to ask the people working on something about issues that trouble them. It has to be like a team game where the objective isn't to criticize the team, but to point out weaknesses so that the team can correct them."

In Blackstone's evaluation of the manufacturing company that used asbestos in its products without exposing anyone to the deadly mineral, the core of the risk came from the financial liability of an asbestos lawsuit. Because most financiers don't know the intricacies of asbestos liability, they extrapolated from the worst cases they had read about in the press. They had insufficient information to make a rational decision. Blackstone, on the other hand, chose to investigate the major driver of the risk, spending a negligible amount compared to the many millions the company would make if it found the way clear to do the deal. Knowledge about the major drivers of a perceived risk allows wise leaders to understand the magnitude of a decision's actual risks and discover options that are both low risk and high reward, by definition taking them into the Profit Zone.

"YOU CAN'T SCHEDULE INVENTIONS"

The valves were the problem.

The Baxter International engineers desperately wanted to shrink the size of their big dialysis machines so that kidney-failure patients could use them at home rather than in the hospital. That meant finding ways to shrink the size and complexity of the valves and tubing and the electrical motors that drove them. But when you're working with machinery that is removing toxins from the blood and organs of someone attached to the machine, you don't take any chances. The valves have to work correctly and safely. To ensure they did, they had to be big and complicated.

Baxter had been an early player in the field of hemodialysis, a process that literally saved the lives of hundreds of thousands of kidney-failure patients. Three times a week, four hours at a time, the patients sat tethered to hulking machines that drew blood from their bodies, cleansed it of toxins that would otherwise kill them, and returned it. The process saved lives, but it took a physical and psychological toll. Patients felt good for several hours after they completed a treatment, but as the toxins accumulated again, they became fatigued, nauseous, and developed headaches. A significant number each year made the fatal decision to give up the treatments.

However, over the years, hemodialysis had become a commodity business, with dialysis centers set up in strip malls, and Baxter had gradually withdrawn from that market. But during the 1980s, Baxter scientists developed a better way to treat kidney-failure patients through a process called peritoneal dialysis. Each day a patient would spend six or more hours lying still as a machine filled the abdomen with dialysis fluid, which absorbed the deadly toxins, then drained the fluid back out. The daily treatments kept the levels of toxins in the body lower so the patients felt better. Baxter had made some headway in persuading nephrologists to use peritoneal dialysis rather than hemodialysis in hospital settings that could accommodate Baxter's big machines. But the key to making peritoneal dialysis more popular and useful, Baxter believed, was to develop a machine that a patient could use at home while sleeping each night. Yet, after many attempts, Baxter's efforts to make a reliable home machine were stymied by the seemingly intractable valve problem. Finally, Baxter CEO Vern Loucks told his engineers to take the problem to Dean Kamen and his DEKA Research and Development Corporation.

Kamen was no stranger to Baxter. Instead of attending classes as a college freshman, he'd spent his days inventing a new syringe pump that could automatically inject a drug over a period of time while the patient sat in a hospital bed. Kamen's Auto-Syringe was a huge success; it allowed chemotherapy and other

patients whose heavy-duty drugs need to be slowly infused into
their bodies to receive the injections automatically, saving nurses
and doctors thousands of hours of shuttling among hospital
rooms injecting small doses of medicine every few minutes. Baxter bought Kamen's start-up company, turning him into a multi-
millionaire at the age of thirty and laying the foundation for
DEKA, his cutting-edge laboratory in New Hampshire.

Kamen isn't afraid to take on some of the world's great engineering challenges. But DEKA usually undertakes such very expensive projects with a deep-pocketed partner who can afford the
multimillion-dollar costs of searching for and developing innovative solutions. Neither Kamen nor DEKA have that kind of money.

So it seemed like just another huge technological challenge
when Baxter came calling. The Baxter engineers told Kamen that
the problem was the valves. They just couldn't make them simpler, cheaper, and more reliable. Could he solve that problem?

"Each of these valves had seventy or eighty parts—motors,
springs, and levers—because if it fails you have to be sure it fails
shut, so it had to have a clutch to release it and close it," recalls
Kamen. "I thought to myself 'Wow, this thing is complicated.'
And there were several of them in every machine. They're noisy
and they're heavy. They said to us, 'Solve our problem. We need
better valves.' "

Kamen's first inclination was to walk away from the project.
"I'm looking at this for a few days and I'm starting to think we
don't need to be spending time on this. They've spent a lot of
time evolving this solution and it's probably about as good as it's
going to get. I doubt we can do any better and, even if we can, it's
going to be an incremental solution because there will still be

several of these things and they're still going to need motors. I've still got this big machine."

But before telling Baxter he couldn't solve the problem, Kamen thought about it some more. Sure, the valves were the root of some of the problems, but there was a more important principle at work. What a person needed, Kamen thought, was a machine that was very small, highly reliable, and extremely easy to use. If DEKA, using Baxter's money and support, could invent a new kind of device with a disposable cartridge that was much smaller, it could then shrink the overall size of the machine to a fraction of the size of Baxter's hospital machines. It was possible to envision a patient simply pressing a button upon going to bed so that the dialysis process took place while the patient slept. Patients might even be able to travel as they wished because they could fit the device under an airplane seat. Such a breakthrough machine could give people with kidney failure much greater freedom to live their lives.

"We went back to Baxter and said, 'Your solution to the problem is to fix the valves, but we think that isn't the real problem,'" Kamen says. "'What the patient needs is a simple machine the size of a VCR with a disposable cartridge that can sit next to the bed. If you restate that as the problem, it would take less time and money to design a new system to solve that problem than to try to fix a system you've been refining for more than a decade.'"

How long would it take and how much would it cost?

A couple of years and a few million dollars, Kamen said.

Loucks told his managers it was a worthwhile risk. If the new device succeeded, the project would yield sizable revenues and have the potential to significantly improve thousands of lives.

Over the next few years, Kamen and his engineering team worked furiously, spending millions of Baxter's dollars trying to make a portable peritoneal dialysis machine. They invented a system that used a small air compressor to control tiny pneumatic valves and membrane pumps, developed new technologies for welding together thin plastic materials, and figured out a way to noninvasively measure and safely move volumes of liquid through the patient. Altogether, the engineers had to come up with many different inventions from scratch. Finally, all the allocated money was spent and Baxter's deadline rolled around. Then came the ultimate blow: DEKA's prototype didn't work.

The frustrated Baxter team called a halt to the project. Kamen recalls their summary judgment: "You said it would take this amount of time. You said it would take this amount of money. We gave you that amount of time. We gave you that amount of money. You're not even close." Baxter didn't believe the technology would work.

Wrong! Kamen argued that DEKA *was* close. The fundamental problems had been solved. Granted, it was taking longer and costing more than anyone thought, but that's the nature of innovation. "You can't schedule inventions," Kamen says. "But at that point we had invented them. It had become just a matter of implementing good focused engineering."

But Baxter was adamant. There would be no further funding for the portable dialysis machine.

Now what? Losing Baxter's sponsorship was a heavy blow. Kamen would either have to kill the project or find another way to continue financing it. But could he find another sponsor? Would the project have to be shelved until someone with money came along to resurrect it? There was one other alternative: Kamen could help finance it himself. But could he muster the money to do that? Should he break his business model that called for deep-pocketed partners?

Kamen thought about what was at stake. The inventions necessary for the portable machine to work now existed. Unlike Baxter, he knew each of the engineers on the team and had full confidence that they knew how close they were to moving from breakthroughs to a complete, working prototype. DEKA had done many successful prototypes of other products and that was really all that was left to do with the dialysis machine. And when the device was completed—not if; there was no "if" involved at this point—Kamen knew thousands of people would have a new lease on life. And there was no question the portable dialysis machine would be in demand by patients. If Baxter didn't want it, another medical device company would. Based on his intimate knowledge of what his team had accomplished so far and on what he knew would be a strong demand for the resulting machine, Kamen committed to going ahead and using his own money.

"It was hard to come up with the money, but it wasn't a hard decision to make," Kamen says. "If the stuff we had invented still hadn't been invented at that point, then I might have said, 'It's not possible based on the current state of technology' and killed it. But I was sitting there with these prototypes saying, 'I know it doesn't look like a finished machine, but we've created all these technologies and now we just have to figure out how to box them up and make an awesome little machine.'"

Kamen told Baxter he intended to push ahead on the dialysis project. If it worked, he said, he would bring it to Baxter first because the company originally had faith in him and had funded the most difficult part of the project. If Baxter didn't want it at that point, he would take it somewhere else.

"It took millions more, and back then that was a lot of money," Kamen says. "I never put the company or my family at risk. That would have been irresponsible. I used royalties from other projects, I quit buying some things I would have liked to buy, I stopped putting money in the war chest to fund other interesting things, and we didn't have great bonuses that year. But I believed that people needed and deserved this technology, that it would be a good thing to do."

Finally, the prototype was finished and Kamen's sponsor reengaged. Baxter took the new portable dialysis machine to the year's biggest nephrology conference in Anaheim, California, where it was displayed at their booth. At first, the doctors who drifted by thought it was merely the control package for Baxter's existing peritoneal dialysis machine. When they learned that it was the *entire* machine, they were awestruck. Baxter was quickly swamped with orders and the HomeChoice peritoneal dialysis machine became a roaring success. Kamen, who owned many patents on the technology, received a higher royalty than he would have received had Baxter continued its full support of the project. Baxter had concerns about the project because the company feared the perceived risks of going forward. Kamen put his own money into the project because he knew the real risks of continuing were very small and that the potential rewards would be very great. By finding a smart risk and investing his own money, Kamen reaped rewards that others had left behind. More important, thousands of lives have been improved as a result.

EMOTIONAL NONSENSE

She was a star, no doubt about it.

Shelly Lazarus seemed to have advertising in her blood. She had enjoyed a meteoric rise as an advertising account manager at Ogilvy & Mather, one of the world's premier ad agencies. Founded by the legendary David Ogilvy, the agency had expanded over the years to generate billions of dollars in billing from offices that spanned the globe. Ogilvy & Mather's stated mission was to build brands, and it had been phenomenally successful at doing that for companies such as Kraft and American Express. Indeed, Lazarus ran the highly lucrative and very-high-profile American Express account, overseeing the print and television advertising that made the company an iconic household name. The only question people at the agency had about her was what she would do next.

It was a question that Lazarus had, too. She knew the standard answer, the one she was supposed to have. "The standard career path within Ogilvy is you grow up in an office and then you go run another office that is of manageable size," she recalls. "If you grew up in New York, you'd go run Atlanta or Houston or you'd go over to Singapore and run the advertising agency there, because in those days advertising was the primary Ogilvy enterprise."

But the standard answer didn't appeal to Lazarus. Her pediatrician husband had developed a private practice in New York and couldn't just up and move to another city. And Lazarus didn't want to move to another city without him. "I couldn't just say, 'See ya! I'll be back in three years,' " she says.

No one was pushing her to move. Her bosses were delighted with her success as an account executive and would have been perfectly happy to keep adding to those responsibilities. Biding her time, Lazarus continued to work on the American Express account, Ogilvy's single-largest advertising account. Amex was also the largest account for Ogilvy Direct, the direct-marketing arm of the agency. But the two arms of Ogilvy worked entirely separately. Advertising, after all, was where the creative talent and energy resided. Direct marketing, in contrast, was the home of technicians who basically sent out lots of junk mail.

But Lazarus questioned the wisdom of that separation. "It seemed to me that what we did on the advertising side, if we did it right, would have a significant impact on how many people responded to direct mail," she recalls. "It just seemed obvious to me, so I actually started to pay attention to it and tried to learn about it. I became fascinated by what they did. I thought that it was so amazing that you could change a color on the outside of an envelope and get a 20 percent difference in response."

As the benefits of having advertising and direct marketing work together more closely loomed in Lazarus's mind, she suggested to her bosses that she take over running Ogilvy Direct.

"People looked at me as if I were crazy," she says. "Why would I be going from the premier organization to one where they had what many considered journeymen, the tacticians? It was like I was going from running Bergdorf Goodman, where all the elegant, smart shoppers go, and going to Wal-Mart, where the working class goes."

Would it really be such a career disaster?

The work direct marketing did intrigued Lazarus, a student of human behavior. "They were always experimenting, doing things like changing the word order of a sentence or enlarging the space where you sign your name, making it twice as big, and seeing what the response was."

She also believed that over time, she would be better positioned to forge closer ties between advertising and direct marketing if she were running the direct-marketing arm. "Because I knew the advertising side, I thought I could really start to integrate the two, to get people to think and work together, because the solution we could bring to clients would be so much more interesting when you had the two parts come together."

And she knew it wouldn't hurt morale at direct marketing to have a star from the advertising side actually *asking* to run the discipline. "Direct marketing didn't have a lot of confidence in themselves," she says. "The very fact that I wanted to lead direct marketing, that I could tell them that 'this is where it's really happening, this is the future' said a lot about their importance."

But what about everybody's opinion that she was about to commit career suicide?

"I just took all of the emotional nonsense out of it," she says, "all the stuff about how it's regarded and people putting their nose up in the air, and I just got to the heart of it. I actually concluded that you had to be a better marketer to be good at direct marketing than to be good at advertising. So I could just push aside all the superficial nonsense about the move and just see that it required a set of skills that would be essential to clients."

In the end, Lazarus pinpointed the real driver of the risk to her career from taking a job in direct marketing. The best way to assess the true risk, she realized, was to ask herself: Would she become less valuable to her clients by spending time in direct marketing instead of advertising? After all, in a services business like advertising, it is one's ability to bring in client work that drives future promotions. And with American Express's global proprietary databases that reveal customer spending habits going back decades, Ogilvy had a powerful tool that could be harnessed to ensure that members got services closely tied to their needs and desires. The answer, she concluded, was that experience in direct marketing would make her more valuable to her many clients, including Avon, Ralston Purina, and Campbell's soup.

Lazarus made the move and remained in direct marketing for four years.[6] When she moved back to the advertising side of the business, she used her new philosophy and cross-disciplinary skills with major clients. As an example, American Express customers not only saw the "Membership has its privileges" campaign in TV and print ads, but also experienced the privileges themselves through the special offers that accompanied their monthly statements. Such a deeper brand experience became the hallmark of Ogilvy's work.

The career move proved to be far more rewarding than even Lazarus had envisioned. Less than ten years after gathering the courage and making the decision to move over to direct marketing, Shelly Lazarus became CEO of Ogilvy & Mather Worldwide, running offices in 125 countries and serving an array of blue-chip Fortune 500 companies.

RULES FOR CONQUERING RISK

Everybody looks for the sweet spot, that situation in which the risks are low and the rewards are high. The trouble is, when an obvious situation like that arises, everyone rushes to it. The result? The rewards are diluted and the risks rise. It is much better to spend the time and make the effort to investigate what appear to be high-risk, high-reward situations. If that's what they really are, you can always back off. But if your investigation reveals that the risks aren't nearly as high as they seem, yet the rewards are still there, you can profit from an opportunity everyone else failed to see.

Rule #1: Identify What Really Drives the Risk

Most of us tend to let conventional wisdom guide our decisions. The problem is that conventional wisdom grows out of the all-too-human tendency toward loss aversion. It sees big risks where there aren't any and thus needlessly raises roadblocks that prevent us from making great decisions. Keep in mind that there are three major reasons that people tend to let risk get the upper hand in their decision making. First, they extrapolate on the basis of insufficient knowledge and wind up reaching the wrong conclusion. Second, they let emotions attached to certain alternatives or outcomes overrule objective analysis that would steer them along another path. Finally, they find psychic comfort in following a herd mentality while ignoring information that would lead to a different decision.

When you're confronted by what seems to be a risky decision, ask yourself two questions: What are the one or two key factors driving the risk? What information do I need to determine how dangerous the risk is?

That's how Steve Schwarzman, Dean Kamen, and Shelly

Lazarus dealt with what appeared to others to be huge risks. Schwarzman used world-class experts to lay aside fears of litigation that had frightened away his competitors. It was, in effect, a small investment to gain important knowledge. Had the answer been different, he could easily have walked away from the deal. Kamen added up what had already been achieved and what remained to be done to create a portable dialysis machine. He determined that even though his deep-pocketed sponsor was pulling out, he could fund it himself with little risk and great reward. He recognized that he had an information advantage developed over years of tackling nearly impossible problems, a perspective on DEKA's capabilities that Baxter couldn't share. And Lazarus looked beyond the conventional wisdom that said she was killing her own career to take what she regarded as an obvious move to boost her value to her clients, a move that led ultimately to the top job in her firm.

Rule #2: Reward People for Taking Smart Risks

Helping your team overcome loss aversion and take calculated risks is a core element in turning risks into competitive advantages. Wise leaders use incentives to encourage people to bring forth new ideas, analyze the risks, and tackle those that hold the most promise for success. The most important incentive is to reward people in whatever way you wish—money, promotions, awards—for simply *making* a smart decision, not on the outcome of their decisions. That way, a manager taking imaginative steps to maintain market share or profits in a tough market or a shrinking economy gets the proper recognition compared to someone less aggressive and innovative who cruises to higher profits in a monopoly market. The point is you have to engineer the risk-taking environment that best suits your own situation, a notion Victor Fung has taken to extremes.

Fung, head of the famed Li & Fung Group, the first Chinese-owned modern-day trading company, has one of the most unusual approaches to finding the right people and putting them in an environment conducive to taking chances. Li & Fung, established by Fung's grandfather one hundred years ago, regularly sources such products as apparel, beauty supplies, and food for thousands of clients throughout the world. Today, the trading business operates in over forty countries and trades over $10 billion in merchandise annually. The company is one of the first multinationals to come out of today's developing regions of Asia.

Fung, together with his brother William, has run the company since 1976. He has organized his company into a series of smaller business units, each of which is centered on sourcing and trading a single product line. Headquarters takes care of finance and information technology.

"We manage the company with a portfolio of about 150 different profit centers," comments Fung. "We open and close product groups with relative ease, because everybody works off the same backbone in terms of the operations support, like finance and IT. So all we're doing is changing the different front-end pieces and everything is plug-and-play, so we have a real overall flexibility in pulling business units out and putting business units in."

Recognizing that most business ideas bubble up from below,

from people who work on the front lines, Fung has pushed entrepreneurship down to the level of his business units. As a result, he and his management team are constantly barraged with ideas for new lines of business. Most he rejects on the spot. But he does select several each year that sound promising, and then he and his team go full speed ahead.

"Let's say we wanted to get into camping equipment—we're now quite big in that—we would just set up a small division to start probing that, and if it doesn't work, then we'll close it down," he explains. "We do that very often. We always say you could hire a consultant and study it to death, and pay a lot of money in the process, or you can just jump in and start running around the track. Now, you know the first time you do it you're going to get into a lot of problems. The second time you do it you'll be a little better, and the third time you do it even better. We believe in doing things by trial and by iteration."

The new profit centers are not always successful. "In any one year, we'll probably open five to ten centers and we'll probably close three, or something like that," he says.

With so much change, it is imperative that Li & Fung has a culture in which people are comfortable with risk and are not afraid to lose. Fung accomplishes this by treating each profit center like a small entrepreneurial unit.

"Each is maybe thirty people doing $30 or $40 million of business, and each is run by a very strong entrepreneur," he says. "We call them 'Little John Waynes.' We imagine John Wayne in the middle of a wagon train shooting at all the bad guys."

The people Fung seeks to run the profit centers are entrepreneurs in their own right, some hired directly into the company and others brought in through acquisition of their companies. But Fung has a cardinal rule that he won't buy any company unless he has met the owner and seen his office.

"Once you walk into a man's office and walk through his company, you then have a very good feel for the culture and the way he does business," says Fung. "You see the body language between his employees and him that tells you how they regard him. You see how the office is set up, how lavish it is, how tightly it's controlled, and you get a feel for how frugal he is and what he thinks is important. One walk through the office tells you immediately more about the person than you can ever find out if he makes a presentation in your boardroom."

It is important for Fung to hire entrepreneurial people, but it is equally important to foster an entrepreneurial environment that encourages them to keep innovating. "We have a corporate culture in which there is very little reputation risk to open and close something. If one profit center doesn't work, the Little John Waynes move on and try another."

Fung realizes that his entrepreneurs could reap huge rewards by running their own start-up companies, so he makes sure that if they're successful they won't be penalized because they work for a big company. "We give them a straight percentage of the bottom line, no questions asked," he explains. "One thing we never do is to cap people's upside."

Not every company can emulate Fung's extreme entrepreneurial environment. Certainly, unlimited upside potential and starting and closing myriad businesses over a short period of time won't work in many business models. But there are few organizations that wouldn't benefit by rewarding people for making prudent decisions that work out poorly. That kind of incentive does more than anything else to help people overcome loss aversion and pursue new opportunities.

Rule #3: Test the Waters Before Taking a Plunge

Not all business decisions need to be made quickly. Sometimes it pays to let a concept simmer for a while, experimenting with an idea before committing fully to it. Experiments limit your downside risk, but not your upside reward. If the experiment fails, you will have minimal losses and learned something. But if the experiment works, you can refine the concept and roll it out with significant rewards. Experiments can be a powerful tool to move an idea out of the Danger Zone and squarely into the Profit Zone, as Orin Smith discovered when he took Starbucks into the drive-through market.

To Starbucks' management team, the very idea of being associated with "fast food" was anathema. That wasn't what Starbucks was about, and anything that hinted at connotations of fast food—drive-through stores, for example—simply weren't up for consideration. Being lumped together with McDonald's and Burger King could destroy the brand that had been so carefully built over the years.

"We didn't want Starbucks to ever be seen as a fast-food place," Smith says. "It wasn't that we were inherently opposed to the idea of drive-through stores, but we put the idea on the back burner. We said we wouldn't try it until we had a sufficient number of stores in the market for customers to understand the Starsbucks experience. The brand was based on a total experience and, as hard as we might try, we didn't believe we could deliver the total experience in a drive-through."

But as the company continued to grow, Smith eventually began to think that perhaps Starbucks had established its brand image sufficiently well that it could at least experiment with a single store. The company tried one and it did well. Over a period of a few years, while focusing mostly on expanding its metropolitan stores, the company built a few more drive-through stores. Each was designed differently, but they all worked.

"We didn't have any experience when we started building the drive-throughs, and we ended up solving a lot of problems, like signage, on a store-by-store basis," says Smith. "When we really started to dig into the numbers, we realized that they were the highest grossing stores we had."

The drive-through stores had the same interior ambience as any other Starbucks and thus appealed to the brand's loyal customer base. But they also attracted a new type of customer who had been neglected in the past: people who for one reason or another didn't want to park their car and get out to buy a cup of coffee. That might be a mother with two small children buckled into car seats, or it might be a businessperson who didn't think she had time to get out of her car and stand in a line. The mother could keep her kids in the backseat and the businessperson could be using a cell phone while sitting in line in the drive-through lane. That expansive new customer base made it important for Starbucks to figure out how to build and run an efficient drive-through store.

"At first, we hadn't been anxious to do them because we were concerned that a drive-through wouldn't give the customer the same experience of coming into a store," Smith says. "There hadn't been a lot of planning done and the first ones were pretty inefficient. We hadn't looked at the flows and how you set up equipment and schedule workers. When we began to think seriously about more drive-through stores, we looked back and learned a lot from the different ways the first stores had solved problems. We realized that the ones we had were more costly to build than they needed to be, far-less efficient to operate than they could be, and the branding wasn't as good as it should be."

Experimenting with the idea transformed what would have been a gamble to a simple exercise of evaluating risk. If the experiments had shown that the additional costs didn't produce sufficient additional revenue, it would be easy enough to end the experiment and return to building nothing but walk-in stores. But the experiments worked. Starbucks found that it cost a few hundred thousand dollars more to build a drive-through store compared to a walk-in store. Think about the implications. Had the company ramped up from the start and built, say, a thousand drive-through stores, it would have had a whopping investment of $200 million or more in stores that might have lost money or hurt the brand. Instead, by experimenting with, say, just ten stores, the company only had $2 million or so at risk. If the drive-throughs didn't work, that would be an insignificant loss. But when they proved their potential, there was nothing to stop Starbucks from rolling out a thousand or more.

Today, up to one-third of Starbucks' new stores opening in the United States are drive-through units. The drive-through stores cost about 15 percent more to build than conventional locations, and the operating costs, as expected, are somewhat higher. But they've proven to be the most profitable stores of them all. If Starbucks hadn't experimented with the concept, risking minimal amounts of money, it might never have found one of its greatest market opportunities.

Experiments should be designed to yield usable results. They should test the feasibility of an idea on a representative sample. Firms tend to try experiments in the most favorable conditions or in a place where they are most likely to succeed. But that kind of experiment produces biased information that might not be applicable across the board. If you really want to test the feasibility of an idea, do experiments on a sample that reflects your overall business. That often means using more than one location, department, or customer.

And when designing the measurements of the experiment, think about failing fast. Figuring how to make something work well may take some time, but you want to know as soon as possible if it won't work. The earlier you can end a failed experiment, the more time and money you have for other pursuits.

Rule #4: Create a Risk-Tolerant Environment

Incentives can encourage people to bring new ideas forward. But how do they get those ideas? Do they get enough of them? People have a natural aversion to being ridiculed and seldom are willing to propose seemingly outrageous solutions to problems. Yet those outrageous solutions may contain the seeds of a whole new approach to tackling a problem. Dean Kamen uses his frog-kissing ceremonies to create an environment that makes people comfortable with risk.

When DEKA's engineers are stymied by a particular problem, Kamen brings them together in a conference room with the ultimate temptation: pizza and beer. Not only are the engineers working on the vexing project there, but so are some others who don't have a vested interest in or emotional attachment to the project. "I like to say, 'The brains that got you into this position are not likely to be the brains that get you out of it,' " Kamen explains.

Then Kamen poses a challenge. He wants outrageous new ideas about the project that go well beyond the normal constraints of time and budget. During the development of the iBOT robotic wheelchair, for example, Kamen wanted his engineers to try to imagine a way for the chair to climb into a car unassisted.

"I set these outrageous goals and nobody knows how to get there," he says. "So I tell them to just try wild things. And since we know we don't know how to get there, we expect most and sometimes all of those wild things will not work."

Typically, the engineers have a week to develop their ideas.

After a week of brainstorming and building working presentations to demonstrate their concepts, the engineers come back together to share their ideas. Some are too expensive or too complicated to be practical. Many concepts simply don't work. But there is no downside to failure. As Kamen explains, "You have to approach it with a spirit of, if it didn't work, it was funny. If it didn't work, I learned from it."

After a round-robin discussion of the problem and the outrageous solutions the engineers develop, Kamen, ever the showman, anoints the engineer who has come up with the most preposterous idea in a "frog-kissing ceremony," named for the princess in the fairy tale who kissed a frog that then turned into a prince.

Kamen believes that frog-kissing ceremonies benefit DEKA's culture in two major ways. First, although rarely, they are a source of new ideas. "I'll be the first to admit that it very rarely happens," he says. "That's why you don't risk your company on it, and you don't risk lots of ego and emotion in it. You want it to be something that if a person tries and fails, there's no stigma attached to it."

More importantly, the frog-kissing ceremonies reinforce for the engineers that DEKA is a place where they can and should pursue some of their more outrageous ideas, as long as they can "fail fast"—with minimal time and expense.

"The trouble is, if you carry the basic human aversion to risk and the need to be predictable and meet schedules into the world of R&D, you're snuffing out the future. You've got to have people check their ego and check their judgment and check their insecurities at the door, and walk in and say, 'So now we get to play in Never-Never Land, so now we get to say stupid, silly things, and we hope that by kissing all of these frogs, one of them, one of them, it's rare, one of them will turn into a prince or princess.' "

The frog-kissing ceremonies are a small investment for DEKA, but they help to create something incredibly valuable: a unique culture that has figured out how to take risks at a small cost and has been able to turn offbeat ideas into lifesaving innovations.

But more important than the ceremony itself is that the easygoing attitude toward risk that is such a central part of the frog-kissing sessions carries over into the day-to-day work of the DEKA engineers, empowering them to come up with new ideas and test them without fear of ridicule or punishment if they don't work. As Kamen notes, "The odds are not in your favor, but if you can fail fast and fail cheap and have a good time and learn stuff and every once in a while one of those frogs turns into something you pursue, it's worth it."

Rule #5: Ask "What Would It Take?"

Good is the enemy of great.

That old maxim gets talked about a lot, but seldom is much done about it. Good is easy. Great isn't. But the leader who can encourage her people to figure out how great is attainable can reap huge rewards, as Shelly Lazarus demonstrated when it came time to set budgets at Ogilvy & Mather, where she was CEO.

Lazarus wasn't interested in incremental goals. Instead, she posed a question to the heads of all divisions of Ogilvy: "What would it take to grow the revenue at twice the rate you're running right now?"

That is a goal many businesspeople would regard as unattainable, and Lazarus knew that. "I didn't tell them that we're going there, I just wanted them to tell me what they thought it would take. I want to see what they're dreaming about so then I can help them be brave."

The senior managers of Ogilvy PR came to Lazarus's office with an answer, albeit one they offered in a very tentative way: To increase revenues 20 percent, they would have to hire four very-expensive people.

"They kept almost apologizing for even suggesting it," she recalls. "I just kept saying, 'No, no, no, I want you to do this. You're

saying it tentatively, but I think you ought to say it strongly, because I support you completely.' "

Assured that Lazarus was on their side, the PR executives
went into more detail. Each of the four would cost Ogilvy on the
order of $500,000, including salary, benefits, and bonus. They
would all be recognized talents in the business with proven track
records of excellence at other firms. But it would still be a risk because Ogilvy had to assume that over the course of twelve
months, the new people would generate enough new business to
justify the outlays. Surprisingly, they already knew the four people they would hire.

"That told me they had been thinking about it a lot and were
confident that it was the right decision," Lazarus says. She did
some quick calculations in her head. Sure, it was riskier than
staying the course, but not by much. The incremental salary expenses were small compared to the potential upside in which advertising and public relations would enjoy the benefits of
cross-fertilization, each producing new business for the other. If
the plan failed, the impact on Ogilvy's financial situation would
be negligible.

"I told them, 'I know it's a risk, and I'm willing to accept it. I'm
not just willing to accept it, I want you to go out there and do it because that's the only way we'll grow. Even if just one of the four
works out, I'm cool.' When I said that, I could see the lights go on
in their faces. 'Hey, one out of four, that's a snap. No problem!' "

The result: "They hired all four people, and three out of the
four worked out brilliantly and they've brought Ogilvy PR to a new
place," Lazarus says. The firm gained new expertise in consumer
products and marketing, and within a year had major assign-

ments from Unilever and Kraft. Public relations became one of Ogilvy's fastest-growing units.

Lazarus's simple question—"What would it take?"—was all that the PR people needed to think about the *right* decision, not the *safe* decision. What if Lazarus had never asked the question nor supported the answer? Ogilvy PR probably would have continued on its course of satisfactory performance and would never have grown as quickly. Getting people out of their comfort zone is an approach that Lazarus has consciously spread throughout the organization. "I want employees to be in a growth attitude so that they experiment," she says. "They have to always be taking a risk, and they have to be okay with risk."

CHAPTER 4

Make Vision Your Daily Guide

Vision or Illusion?

Virtually every company today claims to have a vision, a long-term goal that is supposed to guide its management and employees. But it is easy for idealistic visions to degenerate into mere words on paper, lost in the short-term fog of day-to-day business decisions. Wise leaders know that to make the best decisions you need not only the right vision, but also the discipline to let that vision guide every decision you make, even seemingly innocuous day-to-day tactical choices.

Your vision describes what you and the organization are trying to accomplish. Without it, your company is likely to become an unguided missile, whizzing here and there without a clue about where the target is or how to hit it. Your vision also orders your primary objectives. It becomes the reference point against which you and everyone else in the organization measures what needs to be done and what can be ignored. A great vision can and should be stated simply, but it should also be the foundation from which you derive the specific marching orders for the organization to follow.

Setting and stating primary objectives based on a vision eliminates ambiguity, the uncertainty that consciously or unconsciously surrounds the various options you have when faced with a decision. Sticking to your vision forces you to limit your options to those that are within the "boundaries" set by the vision. Time and resources are allocated only to those initiatives that move the company toward its long-term goals. If employees know that customer satisfaction is a primary objective, they need only look for the option that best satisfies that objective. Without a vision and the primary objectives that flow from it, they might instead be tempted to choose an option that improves profit but hurts customer satisfaction.

If you and your company can follow your vision in making every decision, you'll have two major advantages. First, you'll be much more efficient because you won't waste precious time debating seemingly attractive options that are in conflict with the organization's primary objectives. All you need to ask about an option is whether it furthers the vision. If the answer is no, it isn't really an option.

The second advantage is coordinated decision making. The vision serves as a company-wide synchronization machine that ensures decisions made in various silos across the company fit together as a harmonious whole, bringing coherence to everything the organization is doing.

Vision is long term, but many decisions are made in and for the short term. Consequently, everyone will be tempted frequently to set aside the vision "just this once" to pursue short-term opportunities that aren't an integral part of the vision. Got a shortfall in quarterly revenue? Just add a profitable new account even though it doesn't fit into your vision of the customer base you want. Sure, it may work in the short term, but now you're further away from your long-term goal. And your lack of discipline will become contagious. The vision as guiding light is soon extinguished.

Vision has its rewards. In this chapter, you will see how strict adherence to their visions enabled Dermot Dunphy to bring innovation to the mundane packaging industry, Harvey Golub to reinvigorate American Express, and Bill Reilly to veto an expensive project laden with political patronage.

OUR BUSINESS IS BUBBLES

Talk about being in the right place at the right time.

In 1971, Dermot Dunphy had sold his packaging company and was thinking about what to do next. His friends, the founders of the investment bank Donaldson, Lufkin & Jenrette, asked him to take a look at a small protective packaging company a DLJ partnership owned. The company had just lost its CEO, the result of stumbling financial performance.

Understand that in 1971, the protective packaging industry wasn't exactly a hotbed of innovation. Cardboard boxes and wadded paper about sums it up. But lurking on the sidelines was a little company called Sealed Air, the brainchild of two inventors who a decade earlier had created a textured wallpaper consisting of little air bubbles trapped between layers of plastic. The wallpaper went nowhere, but Sealed Air had changed course and targeted the packaging market with a product called BubbleWrap®.

Dunphy's previous company had been a commodity business that was constantly squeezed between giant raw materials suppliers on the bottom and demanding, powerful customers on the top. Sealed Air was nothing like that. "I decided, when I found Sealed Air, that I kind of woke up in heaven and that focusing on the technological edge, combined with a marketing edge, was the way to control my destiny and control the company's destiny," he says.

When Dunphy took over as CEO in 1971, he was determined that Sealed Air was going to approach packaging in a fundamentally new way. "We had a great opportunity to bring genuine technology to a very mundane industry," he says. "We immediately decided that what we were going to do was sell not a product, but a benefit. We were going to sell protection as opposed to packaging products. The strategic vision was that we were in the business of protecting our customer's products from damage caused by shock, vibration and abrasion. And the bubble was our core business."[1]

Formulating a vision is one thing, executing it quite another. Sealed Air was losing money when Dunphy took over, and the investors who owned the company would certainly want to see some results of his experience in the packaging industry and his managerial expertise.

The first thing Dunphy had to decide was how to build a sales team that could best take advantage of the BubbleWrap opportunity. He knew dozens of top-notch packaging salesmen, the kind who have Rolodexes bulging with the names of good customers.

If he could lure them away from their perches at established companies to join an unknown, unprofitable company, they would give Sealed Air an instant foot in the door of the purchasing departments at hundreds of potential customers. Yet he knew they also would bring with them ingrained ways of doing business: discounts, price cuts, deals.

No thanks. Dunphy's vision of what he wanted Sealed Air to become sent him down a different path.

"We didn't hire anybody from other packaging companies," he says. "We started off with the assumption that we wanted our people to be superior. Somebody from the packaging industry would just bring with him the same old mind-set. Instead, we only hired people just out of school or people who worked at technical companies like Hewlett Packard or superior sales companies like Procter & Gamble. Then we taught them packaging."[2]

Finding and training a cadre of salespeople to sell benefits, not products, was a costly and time-consuming solution, but Dunphy believed it was the only way for Sealed Air to succeed. The sales team would bring a fresh approach, selling promises of protection in an industry in which price had prevailed. Fortunately, the young management team Dunphy inherited had already started down this path. They responded enthusiastically to Dunphy's leadership. "When you are effecting change," Dunphy says, "it helps to get in front of the parade!"

Next came the challenge of keeping the technological edge that allowed Sealed Air to charge premium prices. Dunphy knew from his own experience that R&D was essentially a joke among most packaging companies. They knew what was important: cutting costs so they could cut prices, then doing it all over again.

Conventional marketing wisdom would see BubbleWrap as a built-in advantage to get Sealed Air in the door among new customers. Then it could grab a bigger share of each customer's wallet by offering an expanded portfolio of more conventional products.

And then, of course, Sealed Air would be back in the thick of cutting costs in order to cut prices.

Once again, Dunphy's vision of what he wanted Sealed Air to become steered him in a different direction. He didn't want to compete with anyone in the commodity business. Instead, he saw BubbleWrap as only the first of a full line of package protecting products that would emerge from vigorous R&D. Sealed Air would hire researchers in chemistry and mechanical engineering to develop products that didn't yet exist for customers who knew little or nothing about Sealed Air at that point. And like his decision about the sales force, this solution would be costly and time consuming. But Dunphy knew technology was the only thing that separated Sealed Air from the price-cutters.

The combination of a sales force that understood that it sold a benefit rather than a product and a research and engineering team that applied creativity to what was otherwise a mundane business launched Sealed Air on a course from which it hasn't deviated in more than three decades.

"Every other company in the industry sent people out with catalogs saying 'How many bags do you need? Here's our price.' We sent people out with engineering studies who said 'Let us look at your back room, let us into your factory. We'll show you the economic benefits of adopting our thought processes, our designs, and, of course, our products.'" [3]

Dunphy's vision for Sealed Air was simple and straightforward: to be the best at protecting customers' shipments and to bring cutting-edge technologies to the packaging industry. Early in his tenure as CEO, he translated that vision into seven "strategic principles" that he and his management team applied rigorously to every decision they made:

- Patented, proprietary protective products

- Market leadership in whatever market we decide to participate in

- Technology leadership, because it's the main support of market leadership

- Global operations

- High margins

- Relatively low capital expenditures

- Relatively low labor intensity[4]

Those principles were reflected in Dunphy's approach to Sealed Air's growth. As Sealed Air became an increasingly important and profitable player in the packaging business, investment bankers were constantly bringing him ideas for packaging companies Sealed Air might want to acquire. But they failed to take into account Dunphy's unswerving allegiance to his strategic principles and were met with steady rebuffs because the deals they proposed violated those principles.

By the time Dunphy retired in 2000, his relentless focus on

making every decision according to his vision had paid huge dividends. Sealed Air had more than 350 employees in R&D labs scattered around the world and had developed an array of innovative new products in such diverse areas as food and medical packaging. The unprofitable little turnaround that he joined in 1971 had more than $225 million in net income on more than $3 billion in sales and was generating gross margins of 35 to 38 percent in an industry that typically saw returns in the low twenties.[5] Dunphy's original investors, the DLJ partnership that hired him, saw their holdings rise 8,300 percent over the CEO's three decades of leadership.[6] Packaging may not be a glamorous business, but returns of 8,300 percent certainly are.

TOTO, THIS ISN'T MINNEAPOLIS

Who better than an environmentalist to run the Environmental Protection Agency?

Bill Reilly was widely respected as the president of the World Wildlife Fund and the Conservation Foundation when President George H. W. Bush appointed him to head the EPA in 1989. Little did the forty-nine-year-old administrator realize that one of his first major decisions would be one of the most dangerous.

The Two Forks Dam, a $1 billion project that would provide water for Denver and its burgeoning suburbs, was up for EPA review. As Reilly began to study the proposal, the project had progressed so far that support for it was almost universal despite its staggering price tag. Denver officials and development interests understandably were slavering for the dam. Even Reilly's EPA staff and several environmental groups urged approval, mostly to use the dam as leverage to get Denver to agree to more conservation and efficient use of water. Reilly wasn't surprised when the governor of Colorado called to lobby for approval.

"The governor said, 'Bill, the truth is we don't really need the water yet, but we desperately need the project,' " Reilly recalls. "He said it would bring the whole metropolitan area together because the growing suburbs needed the water. He figured that would get the suburbs to cooperate with Denver on transportation and other issues."

Except for one environmental group, Environmental Defense, everyone Reilly heard from favored the project. As the new head of the EPA, he saw that it would be easy to check "Yes." There would be no second-guessers. Everyone expected an approval.

Then Reilly listened to himself. The project did not square with his vision for environmentally sound development: Sustain, don't change, important environmental areas without a compelling need.

"I had strong views about water use in the West," Reilly says. "I really thought that we needed to enter a new era of water management, rather than water development. Denver has an arid climate. With big projects like this, Denver would just take more and more of people's canyons and free-flowing streams and never adapt its water consumption to its ecology. I just thought it had to stop."

Reilly decided that Colorado's free-flowing rivers, its fish populations, and its scenic canyons should be protected, not changed. He made a tough decision: to invoke the Clean Water Act and stop the development of the Two Forks Dam. Before his announcement he had one more person to see.

"I talked to Senator [Lincoln] Chafee, the ranking Republican on the environmental committee, before I did it. And I said, 'Just supposing I were to make a very controversial use of one section, section 404C, of the Clean Water Act, would I be putting that act at risk in Congress?' And he said, 'Everybody hates that provision up here. I don't need to know what you're planning to do, but I would give you one piece of advice. Whatever you're going to do, do it when we're out of town.' "

It wasn't a strong endorsement, but Chafee's advice was useful. On Good Friday, while everyone was out of Washington, D. C., Reilly announced that the EPA would be reviewing the Two Forks Dam project, an announcement tantamount to vetoing the project, which ultimately he did in November 1990.

"It was a very dangerous decision for me to make," he says. "I remember the night I made it. I didn't know how the president was going to come out. I said to my wife, 'Well, we'll find out now how much he wants to be the environmental president because this is going to really blow up.' "

It did. Suddenly, Reilly was on the hot seat in western papers, the target of angry telephone calls and newspaper editorials. Lee Atwater, the head of the Republican Party, lambasted Reilly in the news media. An angry Colorado senator told Reilly, " 'I won't argue that you destroyed Denver. What you have destroyed is Denver as a city of green trees and parks.'

"I said, 'We're talking about Minneapolis here, aren't we.'

"He said, 'Yeah, it does look a lot like Minneapolis.'

" 'Well, I don't think it should,' I said."

Yet all the apparent hostility concealed some quiet support for Reilly's principled decision. "I went over to see Lee Atwater, the head of the GOP, and he was standing with his back against the wall with his hands up. He said, 'Look, you made so many people so mad with that decision that I just had to attack you.' But he added that 'I've been looking at the mail and it's seven to one in your favor.' "

Reilly got kudos from his staff. "My own water staff gave me advice to approve it, but were thrilled when I vetoed it," he says. "I said, 'Well, why didn't you tell me what you really thought?' They said, 'We just didn't think you'd ever do it. We thought it was too risky.' "

Despite all the Two Forks Dam momentum, Reilly ignored politics and intense pressures and followed his vision to make the best decision in his judgment for the nation. Reilly could have acted like everyone else and told himself to ignore or suppress his values rather than set himself up for a big confrontation. He could have told himself just to let the dam go through, using it as leverage for future initiatives. But Reilly's clear, closely held belief that resources had to be directed to sustain the environment rather than to impair it meant that he stood firm despite being under immense political pressure.

"IN EVERY DECISION I MADE . . ."

When Harvey Golub was named CEO of American Express in 1993, the company was in deep trouble. Golub wanted to shift the once-vaunted company to a brand strategy and away from the vision of a financial conglomerate his predecessor had pursued.

"I thought the brand strategy fit the American Express culture, which was a service-oriented culture throughout all the businesses that we were going to keep and build upon," he recalls. But the challenge was how to craft a vision that expressed to employees, customers, and the world at large what he was thinking in simple, understandable terms.

"We went through months of discussions in Planning and Policy Committee meetings about how to explain it," he says. "It had to be a phrase, not a sentence or a paragraph. We weren't writing the Declaration of Independence. Finally, I just got tired at one of the meetings and I said, 'Let's just call it "The world's most respected service brand." People will get it. It says what we're trying to do, that we're trying to gain respect, not affection or love.' And people got it. They said, 'You know, it makes sense to me, I can understand what you're doing.' "

But to fulfill that vision of making American Express "The world's most respected service brand," Golub knew he would have to guide the company through some big changes. American Express, once a company based on pedigree and prestige, had lost its way when it attempted to diversify its travel-related business by buying an investment bank and a stock brokerage firm. The diversification hadn't worked, and the company's stock was trading at half its prediversification levels.

Golub set about devising the principles that would be the foundation for the decisions that would take American Express toward his vision for the company. "To make decisions efficiently and effectively, one needs to have criteria. And in order to have criteria, one must have principles," he explains.

The three decision-making principles that emerged were simple and easily stated. First, the decision must build and reinforce the brand. Second, it must have a positive impact on customers. Finally, it must incorporate world-class economics.

Using those criteria, Golub made decisions quickly to get American Express back on a course that not only built profits, but also prestige. One of his first major decisions was to sell off the brokerage subsidiary and spin off the investment bank into a freestanding company. For most people, that would have been a difficult decision to make. After all, the investment businesses had the potential to be highly profitable. Worse still, their market value, like their profits, was at a low ebb when Golub decided to pare them from American Express. Had he waited for the financial services businesses to recover before selling them, American Express would have gotten a much higher price.

Golub explains: "In every decision I made I asked myself, 'What effect will this decision have on the American Express brand?' I chose at the outset of my tenure to build a brand strategy. This meant we could not be a conglomerate nor a holding company. We were an operating company. If you have a brand strategy, you cannot have a conglomerate. It must be an operating company. Neither an investment bank nor a brokerage company can be run with values consistent with the American Express brand. The values are so different that it can't be done."

Golub's vision for American Express gave new life to the brand. He took the popular small-business card and expanded it into a wide array of services for small businesses, including auto leasing, travel, preferred rates with shipping and gasoline companies, and even tax advisers. His drive to recruit more merchants to accept the card eventually captured more than 90 percent of all merchant spending, up from just 68 percent who accepted it when he came into office. The American Express Platinum Card became the symbol of prestige in the card business, offering holders special airfare companion programs, hotel upgrades, and access to invitation-only events. Golub introduced hundreds of new consumer cards, tailored to consumers' unique needs and desires, and he turned the American Express subsidiary he previously ran, IDS, into American Express Financial Advisors, yet another component of the company's wide-ranging variety of branded products and services. The financial results reflect his successes: Under Golub, American Express's shareholders gained over 2,500 percent.[7]

RULES FOR MAKING YOUR VISION YOUR EVERYDAY GUIDE

It isn't easy to follow your vision in every decision you make. Dunphy could easily have fallen prey to the urge to build a bigger company, Reilly could have given in to political pressures, and Golub could just as easily have continued to build American Express as a financial conglomerate. But these leaders resisted the temptation, confident that their visions would guide them on a better path that traded short-term gains for long-term gains. To make your vision your daily guide, you need first to ensure you have the right vision, then find ways to articulate it clearly and demonstrate it in action.

Rule #1: Get the Vision Right

When you think about how Dermot Dunphy, Harvey Golub, and John Whitehead, who you met in the Introduction, used vision to drive their companies to new heights of prosperity and prestige, you can see that there are three major tenets that were common to all three leaders' development of their vision.

First, a vision must get people excited. No matter how much you pay them, employees will not give maximum effort unless they are enthusiastic and working for something more than a paycheck. The right vision instills passion in employees to ensure world-class execution. Dermot Dunphy's vision for what Sealed Air would become—a provider of a benefit, not a product—allowed the company to charge high prices for its cutting-edge protective products. That became a tremendous motivation for Sealed Air's sales force.

"In a typical sales meeting, there are lots of war stories about being able to get a price increase accepted or fighting off a competitor who is offering a ridiculously lower price," says Dunphy. "That kind of motivation comes from the vision."

Second, a vision must articulate a worthy goal. A vision's primary value in decision making is to set objectives. This can only occur when a vision tells people what the organization's goals are. Those goals must pass the Goldilocks test: They can't be too easily achieved, nor can they be impossible to achieve. They have to be just right to inspire everyone's best efforts.

When Harvey Golub took over American Express with the avowed goal of making it "the most respected service brand," he knew he needed to set an attainable goal that would inspire the company's employees. The vision he crafted spoke to American Express's service-oriented culture, a proud tradition that had been lost in the quest to expand into financial services. It is a reputational goal, not a numerical goal. Compare Golub's goal to one of becoming the *"biggest* service brand." That's something that a subprime lender might aspire to because sheer size is critical in diversifying the high default risk, but it wasn't a goal worthy of American Express.

Finally, a vision must differentiate your organization. As the cochairman of Goldman Sachs, John Whitehead decided early on that the firm wouldn't join the rush among all its competitors to aid hostile takeovers. Instead, it would stand alone as the firm of integrity, forever differentiated from its competitors in a way its customers valued. Goldman held itself aloof not only because hostile takeovers often didn't work out well, but also because Whitehead believed it was unethical for an investment bank to join forces with a company to take over another against the will of its leaders. That decision was costly in the short run, but it set Goldman apart as the defender of companies under assault. A besieged corporate executive could come to Goldman—and many did—confident that the firm wouldn't use what it learned about the company to later assist another in taking it over. Clients trusted Goldman to always be at their side.

Think carefully about what your company's vision says about the company. Does it excite your people, articulate a worthy goal, and differentiate your company? If the answer to any of those questions is no, you need to rethink your vision. It may just be a dream.

Rule #2: Convert Your Vision into Priority Objectives

A vision that resides solely in the head of a manager doesn't do a company much good. Employees are left to guess where the company is headed and what they need to do to help it get there. That's why is it important for a leader not only to articulate the vision clearly and often, but also to derive from the vision a set of primary objectives that serve as road signs to guide everyone in the organization, much as Dermot Dunphy did when he formulated his strategic principles shortly after becoming CEO of Sealed Air.

Yet even someone as dedicated to following his vision as Dunphy found himself occasionally tempted to take a shortcut. As Sealed Air grew, Dunphy began to see opportunities to expand the business into additional areas by acquiring other companies. One very attractive potential acquisition was a company in Tulsa, Oklahoma, that produced stretch film, which is used to wrap and anchor boxes to pallets. Essentially, the company made industrial-strength Saran™ Wrap.

Excited about the prospect, Dunphy chartered a small jet to ferry the top management team from its New Jersey headquarters to visit the Tulsa company. On the ride home, Dunphy reflected on the day, pleased with what he had seen, and began talking about the next steps to move forward with the deal to acquire what he described as a "decent, high-margin business."

Then Sealed Air's senior vice president in charge of international activities, a key executive in the company, spoiled Dunphy's reverie. He told Dunphy that their trip to Tulsa had confirmed what he already suspected: There was no cutting-edge technology involved in stretch film. To acquire the company, Sealed Air would have to deviate from its long-standing vision embodied in Dunphy's strategic principles.

"He was slightly shocked that I was considering breaking away from our high standards," Dunphy recalls. "He half seriously, half amusingly, but rather bitingly accused me of trying to build a bigger company so that I could boast about it to Harvard Business School friends at my forthcoming reunion. That got the message across pretty clearly!"

Dunphy thought carefully about what the senior vice president had said.

"There was enough impact in what he said that it made me think, 'Well, you know, maybe he's right. I can't totally analyze this, but it's always tempting to build a big business.' If we had wanted to build a big packaging company, it would have been the easiest thing in the world to do," he says. "All the packaging companies were for sale. I could easily have built a $20 billion packaging conglomerate, but it would have been a lousy company. I'd rather build a smaller company that is a premier company."

It didn't take Dunphy long to admit to himself that the Tulsa deal would only be "for personal aggrandizement, personal ego, and wouldn't be sticking with the discipline." Sealed Air dropped the deal.

Dunphy's articulation of the seven principles armed his employees with the power and the tools to use the company's vision in making every decision. His vice president's invocation of the principles to steer Dunphy back to the straight and narrow path solidified the strength of Sealed Air's vision.

Rule #3: Stay Flexible

A vision to guide you and your organization is absolutely critical for keeping everyone focused on the right goals and how to reach them. But execution to achieve a vision isn't necessarily a straight path. Rather, the execution must evolve over time, recognizing what has been accomplished, what remains to be done, and how circumstances, both internal and external, are changing.

Harvey Golub likens the challenge of keeping a flexible approach to achieving a vision to grooves and ruts. Grooves are good because they keep the company on track. But when the grooves become so deeply worn that they become ruts, a company can no longer change.

"If you look at every leading company that has ultimately lost, one of the things that will be consistent in all of them is that what was a groove has become a rut and ultimately becomes a cultural impediment for even thinking differently," he says.

When Golub took over American Express, the company clearly was in a rut. To get out of that rut, he had to change the organizational mind-set. "I knew that things would change and that I couldn't anticipate many of those changes," he explains. "What I could do is work to ensure an organization that was supple enough to identify things early, or identify the need to create change itself. To get in a groove, I needed organizational suppleness that wouldn't become a rut."

Golub's experience as a consultant at McKinsey gave him some important insights into how grooves become ruts based on organizational structures. "When I was at McKinsey, if someone told me they were organized by geography, I knew what problems they had were centered in products and functions," he says. "If they were organized by product, I knew the problems were geography and function. Whatever way you choose to organize, you will create other problems. So one of the principles is you change. As an organizational principle, what you want to do is move a company among product, function, and geography periodically so that you don't turn grooves into ruts."

While Golub believes that his vision for the American Express brand will remain intact for years to come under new leaders, he's also confident that the vision will be adaptable to new circumstances because of the organizational suppleness he created.

"It's all about what has to be modified," he says. "Just because we did it that way when Harvey was here doesn't mean it's the right thing to do today or maybe even the right thing to think about. You don't just change the structure; you also have to change the thinking and the premises to challenge yourself. If I were going to design a company to put American Express out of business today, what would that company be and let me become that company first."

Singapore prime minister Lee Hsien Loong shares Golub's flexible approach to achieving a vision. "It's always a work in progress, it's always unfolding," he says. "We couldn't predict 9/11, and before that we couldn't predict the Asian financial crisis. You don't know which way the world is going to go."

Singapore has long strived to be the preeminent center in Asia that attracts foreign firms and nationals. As the country's GDP has grown and thus its wages have gone up, it has had to change how it executes that vision. It first made its name in shipping, then manufacturing, then banking, and now is getting into biotech. In order to be able to change the industry of focus that is required from a rising GDP, Singapore's workforce must be flexible. And in order to be flexible, workers have to be well rounded, educated, and willing to be reeducated in a new area.

"You might not know what the future will bring, but you want to be prepared for it, to respond to it, and to take advantage of the opportunities that come along," says Lee. "Your people must have the skills so they can work in a wide range of jobs—and not just the skills, but the mind-set that will allow them to work in a wide range of jobs."

That kind of preparation begins with basic education that teaches not just skills, but also how to think, adapt, and work with others, says Lee. Beyond basic education, the ability to be flexible requires Singapore to offer a wide array of higher-educational options, ranging from universities to technical schools.

"You can start off in the Institute of Technical Education, which is very much hands-on, but you can then go on to get a university degree if you wish," he says. "It makes the system flexible and it also keeps our society open."

Lee shares Golub's views about organizational suppleness, too. In Singapore's case, that means the government has to not only encourage flexibility, but practice it as well.

"You don't want to have the same person or the same team having the same role for a very long time because they become set in their ways," he says. "You have to change the ministers, bring in new people and new ideas. It's always a risk because you might not think a young person is ready yet, but you have to keep moving." Under Singapore's rules, top civil-service officials can keep one job for five years and are then allowed to take another top job for another five years. After that, they must step down to clear the way for new officials.

"It means they retire quite early, often in their early fifties," Lee says. "We lose people who are still useful to us, but if we didn't do that, I think you would find some people who have stayed longer than they should."

CHAPTER 5

Listen with Purpose

Are you listening carefully?

Then you're missing the point.

It isn't *how* you listen, it's *why* you listen that's important.

If you're like most people, you go into a meeting and put on your usual listening act. You shut the door to avoid distractions, you look the person in the eye, you take a few notes, and you repeat what they've said every so often. The message is clear: You're listening carefully.

But you almost certainly aren't listening with purpose, and that is the fundamental key to listening. Before you walked into that meeting, did you have a clear idea about why you would be listening to the other person? Don't worry, few people do. In fact, the wise leaders we interviewed didn't even realize they listen with purpose until it became clear in one interview after another. They almost unconsciously prepare themselves for each meeting by thinking through why they are asking for that person's opinion. That way, they're prepared to make the most of the interaction, taking away from it knowledge and impressions the other person had no idea he was conveying. As you'll see, the ability to listen with purpose not only results in great decisions, but it also results in great *execution* of those decisions.

At the most fundamental level, we identified three major purposes leaders have for listening. The first is listening to gather information. But we don't mean just any information. You must be listening specifically to fill in gaps in the information you already have. That means thinking carefully about what you already know and what more you need to know before you even go into the meeting. It also means seeking out the right people to listen to, as Orin Smith did when he was thinking about taking Starbucks into smaller towns and rural areas.

You also need to listen with the purpose of learning how to communicate. People engaged in a candid discussion in an environment in which they do not fear retribution will almost always reveal the things that they are worried about or that are most likely to motivate them. Your job is to listen to the dialogue to identify those "hot points" that emerge so that when a decision is ultimately made, you can address the fears and concerns of those who were opposed and rally to you those who support the decision.

Finally, listen with the purpose of generating ownership. A great decision that can't or won't be executed is no decision at all. In the run-up to an important decision, very few people want the responsibility of making the decision themselves, but they want to know their point of view is heard and considered. Listening to their various viewpoints assures them that their input is valued, and that goes a long way toward generating buy-in for the final decision.

Listening with purpose showed Vern Loucks whether to split off his "baby," laid the groundwork for Singapore prime minister Lee Hsien Loong to overhaul his country's retirement system, and helped Bill Reilly launch an effort to rescue the world's oceans.

WE'RE YOUR BUSINESS, SO GET OUT OF OURS!

Vern Loucks considered it one of his best moves.

As the CEO of Baxter Healthcare, Vernon Loucks was rightfully proud of his company's success. Since he took over as CEO in 1980, Baxter had enjoyed phenomenal growth. Its 120,000 products could supply 70 percent of any hospital's needs.[1] But in 1987, Loucks had seen a growing problem confronting Baxter: skyrocketing health-care costs were driving insurers to reduce expensive hospital stays in order to hold down their own costs. The solution, Loucks decided, was to shift some of Baxter's emphasis to alternate site care. A company called Caremark, a pioneer in the home-infusion market, seemed like the perfect vehicle to help Baxter make the transition. Baxter took the plunge, purchasing Caremark for just over half a billion dollars.

Sure enough, Baxter's acquisition of Caremark paid off handsomely. Under the leadership of veteran Baxter vice president Lance Piccolo, Caremark quickly became the star of Baxter's new alternate site division. Working with doctors, Caremark sent its nurses and clinicians to see patients in their homes, or at other sites to administer drugs and respiratory therapy and monitor patients' conditions. The service was particularly appealing to the growing number of elderly who found it difficult to leave their homes to go to a doctor's office. Caremark's explosive growth generated huge profits for Baxter. Thrilled with Caremark's results and proud of his role as the architect of Baxter's alternate site strategy, Loucks dubbed Caremark "one of my babies."

"It turned into a lot more than any of us thought it was going to be," he says.

But it didn't take long for Baxter's hospital clients to notice that they suddenly had a new competitor: Baxter!

"As we became successful—and we became *very* successful— our hospital customers said, 'Hey, wait a minute, those are our customers. Patients are our business, not your business. We're your business. And if you value your business, then get out of ours,'" Loucks recalls.

Now Loucks had a real problem. Caremark was one of the biggest growth platforms at Baxter, and with the inevitable shift to alternate site services, it was a unique opportunity for Baxter to be a leader in a fast-growing market. Yet hospital customers were telling Baxter's sales force they would switch suppliers if Baxter kept competing for their patients. Should Baxter continue to focus on alternate site business and risk its hospital business, or should Caremark be spun off as a stand-alone company?

Billions of dollars were at stake, but Loucks wasn't yet ready to make a decision. Caremark was his baby, so on a personal level he would like to keep it. But deep in his gut, Loucks suspected that a spin-off might make more sense. After all, the company's shareholders would still own both entities, and he was putting about $4 billion in hospital sales at risk by keeping Caremark as part of Baxter.

To help him envision Baxter's future and answer that critical question about Caremark, Loucks summoned 135 of Baxter's top managers to a retreat in Alaska.

Alaska!?

Loucks picked the site on purpose: "I thought it provided a relaxed atmosphere where people could do things totally unrelated to their day-to-day business, but at the same time consider a fairly significant piece of their strategic future." And while Baxter only had a dozen or so senior managers, Loucks thought it important that many more who had a vested interest in the future of Caremark and Baxter, including sales managers, have some input into the decision-making process.

In Alaska, Loucks divided the executives and sales managers into small groups to do strategic reviews and thoroughly discuss the alternatives and implications for Baxter, Caremark, and, significantly, for their own careers. "The idea was to get everybody on the same wavelength in terms of what top management was thinking about and to get their input," he explains. He moved from group to group, listening carefully to what different people were saying.

It quickly became obvious that no consensus would emerge from the discussions. The hospital sales force was demoralized. "The guys who were dealing with our hospital customers were pretty battered," Loucks recalls. He vividly remembers one Texas-based sales manager grimly tallying the losses in hospital purchases his sales force was experiencing and predicting that it would only get worse.

But those in favor of keeping Caremark had a much rosier view of the world, and not surprisingly. Alternate site care was basically a mom-and-pop business. Caremark already had the largest market share in the home-infusion industry at 20 percent and was looking at a huge opportunity to consolidate the fragmented industry. It also was aggressively growing a nascent business in prescription delivery with the potential to be orders of magnitude larger than its existing business. They were puzzled why Baxter would want to just let them go. "They felt that we're just getting to the point where Caremark was really taking off," Loucks says.

Faced with a divided organization, Loucks knew that whatever his decision, he would have to explain it in a way that gave everyone the confidence and the motivation to execute it well.

"These guys are all pretty strong guys, and when you ask them a question, they're going to give you a straight answer," he says. "What I was looking for was 'What's the organizational support for this?' I knew I might have to make a decision that would be contrary to the flow, but I also knew that if I'm going to do that, I want them to understand why I'm doing it."

After the passionate discussions in Alaska about Baxter's future, Loucks decided that his baby needed to leave home. If Caremark remained part of Baxter's portfolio, it threatened to harm the business of the world's preeminent hospital supply company. If it were spun off, Baxter's shareholders would still own it, but the two companies would not stand in the way of each other's progress. There would no longer be one company with competing internal agendas.

"The decision ultimately came down to the fact that the growth of the Caremark business would go on whether we owned it or not, and it may go on even better if it's cut free and allowed to float on its own," Loucks explains.

Despite the sharply divided opinion about what Loucks should do, once the decision was made, there was no resistance. "After we made the decision, there was nobody who asked the question 'Why did he do that?' There may have been some people who wished that we hadn't, but they all knew why we did. It went as smooth as silk."

The Caremark subsidiary went public on December 1, 1992, when each Baxter shareholder received stock in the new Caremark entity. The value of the spin-off was just under $2 billion, a substantial increase from the original $528 million purchase price just five years earlier.[2] Loucks's purposeful listening not only brought him to the right decision, it also allowed him to engage his managers in the decision and communicate why it was made in a way that motivated a divided organization to execute with great success.

EVERYBODY'S MONEY

Ever touched a hot stove burner?

You probably haven't made that mistake again.

Yet here was Prime Minister Lee Hsien Loong, the leader of Singapore, one of the world's most prosperous nations, getting ready to touch that hot burner again. Intentionally.

When Singapore's government tried once before, in 1984, to reform the country's Central Provident Fund—the functional equivalent of the U.S. Social Security system, but based on fully funded personal savings accounts—it ignited cries of pain from nearly everyone, including employers, workers, and the elderly. The government quickly backed off and left the system alone.

Now, despite incremental changes over the years, serious reform was needed even more urgently. Improved life expectancy was threatening to undermine the CPF. When the CPF was originally set up in the 1950s, the average Singaporean lived sixty years. If someone worked until age fifty-five, his accumulated lifetime savings need only last on average five years. By 1984, when the government tried to push through a change that would have advanced to age sixty the point at which workers could tap into their accumulated contributions to the CPF, life expectancy had already grown to more than seventy years of age. By 2006, life expectancy was eighty years, and elderly Singaporeans were beginning to exhaust their CPF accounts. The system had to change. Singapore simply couldn't condemn its elderly poor to destitution. They were the generation that lifted Singapore up from Third World to First World status.

But *how* would the system have to change? Lee, who was educated with honors at Cambridge University and was Singapore's youngest brigadier general, knew he could impose his own ideas if he thought it necessary, and he leaned toward creating a private pension system as the best solution. Yet he also knew that whatever the decision, he would be upsetting several constituencies. Businesses were intent on maintaining their competitive edge in the global economy, and any changes that raised their costs would bring howls of protest. Unions representing workers would want higher contributions from business and had long been pressing for an extension of the retirement age so their members could work until they were older. And Singapore's elderly were growing increasingly worried about outliving their savings, yet didn't want to put off the age at which they could tap into their CPF savings.

"It's a supersensitive subject, first because it affects everybody's money," Lee says. "Second, these are personal accounts, so it's all the more painful for people, who think, 'It's my money, give it back to me now.' And third, that one attempt in 1984 to delay the withdrawal age by five years, from fifty-five to sixty, nearly brought the house down."

The trick would be to fashion a system that spread the burden of reform equitably among the various constituencies so that no individual group would feel singled out to surrender too much. To do that, Lee knew he needed to listen carefully to each constituency, as well as to his own government advisers, to figure out not only what was most important to each group, but also what the government could afford to do.

First stop, the various government ministries that could offer expert advice and make recommendations. The prime minister put together a group of representatives from different ministries, including many bright young men and women, to study various issues such as demographic trends, estimates of return on various investments, and possible ways to restructure the CPF, including the pros and cons of switching the entire retirement security program to a private pension plan. Lee took on the role of first among equals, encouraging his colleagues and associates to speak out forcefully and without fear about any concerns they had. As the prime minister listened to their expert opinions, it became evident to him that his private plan wouldn't work. A private plan, his advisers told him, would put the onus on people to manage their funds themselves, something those with low incomes were not well equipped to do. And when everyone agreed that extending the point at which a person could begin to tap his CPF account was a basic goal, there was one objection.

"One of the youngest of the ministers, said, 'You know, this is going to be very difficult on the people who are in their fifties, because they are the ones who are nearly at the point when they are hoping to take their money out, and just as they're reaching the target, we're moving the glass away. So how about a little bit of sweetener for these people so they feel that you're helping them make this transition?' "

Second stop, the employers, all of whom were concerned about maintaining their competitive position in the global market. Yet listening to them enabled Lee to pick out some very specific hot points. First, the employers knew their workers wanted to stay on the job longer, rather than retire at the mandated age of sixty-two But they told Lee that older workers often were not as productive as they once had been, and they also had higher medical costs than young employees. What's more, they said, if older workers held on to their senior-level jobs longer, it would be difficult to promote ambitious young employees.

Next stop, the unions that represented many of Singapore's workers. Over the years, Lee had established a rapport with many union leaders, often inviting them to lunch or tea to discuss various issues affecting workers, and he knew they would be candid with him. As he expected, the unions were all for extending the official retirement age. But as he listened to them, it became clear, too, that they knew their older members weren't as productive as they had been and that employers would strongly resist any efforts to force them to keep older workers on the payroll. They were eager for ideas about how best to overcome that resistance through some compromise proposal.

Finally, what were older Singaporeans thinking about work and retirement? Lee had to listen carefully to understand their concerns in order to communicate how the changes he wanted to make would affect them. To do that, as well as to get a preview of what Singapore might look like in the year 2020, Prime Minister Lee visited Radin Mas, a district in which nearly one person in six is sixty-five or older, compared to the one in twelve in Singapore as a whole. Radin Mas's demographic profile is where Singapore will be in twelve years. As he listened to the elders, Lee once again identified two hot points: employment opportunities for older workers and having sufficient funds for old age. One woman of sixty-seven put it bluntly to Prime Minister Lee: "My CPF runs out this year. What happens after that?"

He could only tell her that the government was working on the problem.

Amid all the consultations, the prime minister was careful not to be too specific about what he and his team of government experts were thinking. "You can't go around asking, 'Do you prefer this particular scheme or that scheme?' People don't have informed views on how to design a social security system," he explains. "You have to think about how you're going to present it and persuade people to come along."

But he was gratified to find that the people with whom he consulted understood the nature of the problem confronting

Singapore. A woman representing one of the labor unions told him, "It's not going to be very popular, but you have to do it. I know this. I was young, I paid no attention, and only when I had two children did I start doing financial planning for my old age."

"She's telling her people this is going to have to happen, so let's see how we can massage the package to make it more acceptable," Lee says. "So that's reassurance to me that it's saleable."

Still, the days leading up to the unveiling of the new CPF provisions were tense. Just a few days before details were to be released, the *Straits Times,* Singapore's national newspaper, released a poll that showed heavy support for working to an older age and for increased returns on personal savings in the CPF system.[3] But when asked if they favored an increase in the age at which people would withdraw their funds from the CPF, the answer was a resounding "No!"

Finally, on August 19, 2007, Prime Minister Lee used his annual National Day Rally speech to unveil the result of the many interviews, meetings, consultations, and studies about how to reform the CPF. To help sell the reform program, he illustrated the speech with photographs taken during his visit to Radin Mas, painting a picture of what Singapore will look like in 2020.

The new plan addressed the various hot points that each group had voiced, granting concessions to offset the pain.[4] While the official retirement age remains sixty-two, employers will be required under new reemployment legislation to offer workers a new job at age sixty-two. It may be a less-senior job and at a lower rate of pay, but at least an employee won't be forced out. And to provide incentives for older people to work and for employers to hire them, a negative income tax will offer workers a wage supplement of up to 25 percent of their salary. To help the poorest Singaporeans, the interest rate that the government pays on each employee's required savings in the CPF will rise modestly on the first $60,000. But the biggest change of all was the extension of the age at which workers can draw down their CPF funds, to sixty-five from sixty-two. Workers in their fifties who suddenly saw access to their nest eggs receding three years into the future were given bonus interest payments on their savings to help mitigate the impact.

The sweeping plan to reform the CPF was broadly accepted. There would be some fine-tuning to do as the various changes were implemented, but because Prime Minister Lee invested large amounts of time and effort listening to his various constituencies' concerns and weighing them against what he thought the government needed to do to ensure the long-term viability of the CPF, he was able to convince his fellow citizens that if they all shared a little pain, Singapore would continue to have a healthy economy with no one left behind.

ENLISTING THE DOLPHINS

The oceans were dying and the world didn't seem to care.

Bill Reilly was rightly proud of the accomplishments of the World Wildlife Fund. Over three decades, the WWF, the world's largest privately financed conservation organization with more than 4 million members, was able to number among its successes saving endangered species, protecting threatened habitats, curbing pollution, and preserving disappearing wetlands. But as the twenty-first century dawned, Reilly, chairman of the WWF, was concerned that there remained a vast frontier where the WWF had been largely absent: the world's oceans.

"We hadn't applied to the oceans the same priority or the same urgency as we had to other problems," he says. "We hadn't been paying enough attention to it, and it turns out the situation was fairly dire."

The biggest problem that he and his officers saw was overfishing. The statistics on plummeting fish populations were grim. From cod to swordfish to giant bluefin tuna, the arrows all pointed toward eventual extinction at current harvest rates. And destructive fishing methods such as explosives and poisons were also destroying the world's coral reefs. Fish and coral, though, were things that pretty much remained out of sight and out of mind for most of the population. Only someone attuned to the problem could see the evidence right there in the grocery store. Wild Atlantic salmon, one of America's favorite fish, returns from the ocean to its native rivers to spawn. Today, it is extinct in 84 percent of its native rivers.[5] Reilly noted that in grocery stores and restaurants, the vast majority of salmon for sale was farmed fish. He heard from chefs that wild fish like salmon and swordfish in the markets were getting smaller. "We're getting smaller fish because we're moving down and getting younger fish," he explains. "Older fish that reproduce are becoming increasingly rare."

And Reilly knew the problem was only going to become worse as populations of developing countries grew and governments— particularly the European Union and the Japanese—increased their financial subsidies to their fishing industries.

"The public doesn't understand that the area that's covered by the earth's oceans supports two billion people economically," says Reilly.

The WWF decided to create a new priority: to preserve the fragile ecosystems of the world's oceans.

But how to generate concern among the general public? The oceans were simply too far removed from peoples' everyday lives. Few consumers worried about overfishing when Chilean sea bass was readily available at almost any nice restaurant. Reilly needed a new way to communicate the WWF decision to capture the public, and he had to find it quickly.

Reilly set out to listen, not just to his environmentally aware constituents, but to the man and woman on the street. Distilling information from myriad town meetings, letters, and conversations, Reilly reached a seminal conclusion: Coral reefs, endangered sea creatures, and shrinking fish filets struck dull chords with the public. But what did get attention were lovable animals. On land, it was baby seals, fawns, and lion cubs that tugged at heartstrings. In the oceans, the most lovable animals were the cetaceans, the dolphins and the whales. Everyone loves dolphins for their playfulness and intelligence, and people are awestruck by the magnificence of whales. The public related to these animals they knew from their youth, and they were concerned about their futures. As a start, Reilly knew he could crowd the theater for protecting the oceans if he advertised his leading performer, the dolphins.

In July 2002, the World Wildlife Fund announced a narrow but highly strategic mandate: Reduction of entanglement of dolphins in fishing nets would be a top priority of the organization. Reilly explains why dolphins, themselves mammals, became the poster child for declining fish stocks: "One of the emotional deals you can make that really does get people is cetacean bycatch. The reality that you're killing a lot of porpoises, simply to catch fish that you and I eat, and you're drowning them—that's the way to get people to worry about this."

By listening to the audience he wanted to capture, Reilly learned that communicating the WWF's decision to shift conservation efforts to the oceans had to start with dolphins and whales. "We decided to hit cetacean bycatch, because it's something that's correctable, but it's also something that is very directly of concern to people when they understand it, because people really like whales and dolphins."

Reilly engaged and motivated the broader public with a targeted message that ignited passion. Wise leaders listen carefully to discover the words and issues to which their audiences will respond. Like Reilly, they use these ideas to engage their audiences in their decision and to win their help on its execution.

RULES FOR LISTENING WITH PURPOSE

Listening is all about learning. But listening with purpose requires you to place what you hear in the right context. The person to whom you're listening may think he's communicating a very specific point, but if you're listening with purpose—prepared to fill in the gaps in your own information, to identify hot points that will need attention when you communicate, and to generate ownership—you are probably hearing something else. It's up to you to interpret what you're hearing and put that information in its proper place within your decision-making process.

Rule #1: Ask the Right Questions

To get the right answer, you have to ask the right question. Too often the decision-making process starts when a single event or person raises a narrow question that isn't the right question. But once that ball is rolling, it becomes hard to break the momentum and reconsider the question that got it all started. The result may be the right answer, but to the wrong question. What we really need is the right answer to the right question. Wise leaders know that the way a problem is framed has a lot to do with how it is solved. They listen carefully to gather information, but in the end it is their responsibility to distill all that information and decide what the problem really is.

In 2000, General Motors' Oldsmobile brand was 103 years old and sported an impressive history of innovation. In 1926, it introduced chrome trim to the American motorist. In 1940, you could order your Series 60 sedan with a Hydra-Matic automatic transmission, the first fully automatic transmission offered in large volumes. In 1949, it was the introduction of the Rocket V-8, the world's first high-compression eight-cylinder automotive engine. In 1966, the company brought consumers the Toronado, the first mass-produced front-wheel-drive car from an American manufacturer. And who among the muscle car buffs of the 1970s doesn't have fond memories of the 4-4-2, one of the hottest of the genre, its designation derived from its key attributes: a four-barrel carburetor, four-speed transmission, and dual exhausts?

Alas, in the mid-1980s, Oldsmobile began to run out of gas. Unit sales slipped below 1 million in 1987 as consumers turned increasingly to more stylish and reliable foreign cars.[6] For the next thirteen years, Oldsmobile fought a rearguard action, becoming increasingly desperate to find salvation. Its traditional customer base—older white males—was literally dying off. A catchy new advertising slogan—"This Isn't Your Father's Oldsmobile"—only served to drive home the point that Oldsmobile appealed to the wrong demographic. In the mid-1990s, Olds launched its biggest effort yet to regain relevance, spending over $3 billion to revamp the Oldsmobile lineup to make it more appealing to younger buyers, including the introduction of the Alero small car and the Aurora, a powerful, pricey sedan intended to compete with such luxury models as BMW, Mercedes, and Lexus.[7]

Rick Wagoner knew all about Oldsmobile, both its legacy and its problems, when he became, at age forty-seven, the youngest CEO of General Motors. The rising young executive knew that one of his biggest challenges would be to figure out how to revive Oldsmobile.

There was a lot at stake for GM. At the time there were twenty-eight hundred Oldsmobile dealers who depended on having good cars to sell to pay their employees, rents, and taxes. Sixty-three of those dealers were exclusively Oldsmobile dealers.[8] They were eagerly awaiting Wagoner's new plan to boost Oldsmobile's sagging fortunes.

As the CEO of the world's largest automaker, Wagoner could muster enormous resources to figure out a future for Oldsmobile, including his own diverse experience as a finance expert, head of GM's operations in Brazil, and chief of the company's North American operations. He listened intently to ideas from every source. Some of the options were little more than the standard gimmicks Detroit had been using for years to "move the iron," including no-down-payment financing for consumers. Others were more innovative, notably sourcing new Oldsmobile models from GM's foreign operations. In October, Oldsmobile invited advertising agencies to pitch concepts for new advertising campaigns. There was no shortage of ideas to revive Oldsmobile.

But amid the debate about how to revive the Olds brand, Wagoner was also being bombarded by a litany of problems confronting the brand in 2000. Sales were still falling despite the billions invested in new products. The marketing department projected that Oldsmobile would sell fewer than three hundred thousand units in 2000.[9] Karen Francis, Oldsmobile's general manager and a whiz who had made her name as a marketer of toothpaste and pencils, resigned. The customer base remained heavily skewed toward white males over fifty. Oldsmobile may have been a legendary source of automotive innovation, but at this point it was a very sick puppy.

Wagoner felt the weight of tradition pressing him to revive Oldsmobile. But the more Wagoner thought about it—balancing the ideas for revival against the mounting tally of problems—the more he began to think that everyone was asking the wrong question. It isn't what we do to revive the marque, he decided. It was whether Oldsmobile should be closed down.

The answer wasn't easy.

"It was a tough decision because in my mind the facts of the case were so clear," Wagoner recalls. "But the sentiment, the emotional aspects of it, the implication for so many groups, was so big. We'd given it a hard try, we brought out a whole new range of products, spent a lot of money, and it wasn't working. Nobody under fifty wanted to own an Oldsmobile. So it was clear to me that that was a bad use of money. I'd rather take the money and revive Cadillac and bring out Hummer and stuff like that, but it was a very hard thing to do. Oldsmobile had just celebrated its one hundredth anniversary. One hundred years of tradition isn't to be taken lightly."

On December 12, 2000, Wagoner announced that GM would phase out the Oldsmobile line over the next few years.

The decision created angst among customers and dealers. But most knowledgeable observers applauded the move as a necessary step to focus GM's money, time, and energy on its remaining product lineup. The supporters included the person who Wagoner respects and appreciates more than almost any other, Jack Smith, his boss and mentor. "I'm not sure what he wanted me to do, but he supported the decision 100 percent," Wagoner says. "It was a huge splash when it happened and a massive trauma for about six months, but we're over it."

Wagoner listened to a lot of input about ways to revive Oldsmobile, but in the end what he heard was that the line couldn't and shouldn't be saved. GM had other priorities that were more important and more likely to succeed. By reframing the nature of the debate from "how to save Oldsmobile" to "should we save Oldsmobile" he set the stage for a traumatic but needed decision. As a result of Wagoner's purposeful listening, GM is no longer pouring good money after bad trying to prop up a dead brand. The reallocation of resources has begun paying big dividends with two models—the Cadillac CTS and the Chevy Malibu—drawing rave reviews in their latest incarnations. *Motor Trend* magazine, citing the CTS as "the star of a new GM revival," named it the 2008 Car of the Year. The CTS has even begun to attract younger buyers, something that Cadillac had tried, but failed, to do for years.

It's easy to let events or other people dictate the agenda for making decisions. Only through careful listening can a wise leader discover that everyone is arguing about the wrong thing. Reframing the debate to bring forward the right question can lead to breakthroughs that alter a company's future course.

Rule #2: Challenge Assumptions

We all make assumptions, even scientists. They call their assumptions "hypotheses," and they do carefully controlled experiments to prove or disprove their hypotheses. Too often in business we make the assumptions, but don't test them thoroughly. That can lead to bad decisions, as Bill Reilly learned the hard way.

Reilly really didn't want to start a trade war. After all, he was the head of the Environmental Protection Agency, not an agency often associated with trade disputes. When Reilly's staff alerted him that they had found a fungicide called procymidone in imported wines, Reilly at first didn't think much about it. He assumed they meant wines from a specific vineyard or a certain producer.

But no, it was much bigger than that. The staff had found the chemical in 20 percent of French wines and 10 percent of Italian and Spanish wines slated to be imported to the United States. All told, it amounted to $500 million of wine imports.

That was a problem. Reilly sat down with the members of his staff who knew the most about procymidone to figure out a response.

"Has the manufacturer of the fungicide applied for a tolerance and presented the data to justify it?" Reilly asked.

"No, and what little we know about the chemical indicates it wouldn't get one if they did," was the answer: There was no tolerance.

With the public's health apparently at stake, Reilly felt he had to make a fast decision.

"It seemed pretty clear what I had to do," he recalls. "I said, 'No tolerance, huh? All right, impound all the wine that hasn't yet been shipped to the United States.' The staff said, 'Are you really going to do that?' I said, 'That's the law.' So we did. And I did it fairly quickly, and I told the White House and the secretary of agriculture what I had done."

Reilly was under no illusions that his decision was going to go unnoticed. You don't just ban half a billion dollars' worth of wine from proud wine-producing nations like France and Italy and not hear about it. It didn't take long for the fireworks to start.

"The French went crazy," Reilly says. The French ambassador stormed into Reilly's office in record time. At first, he suggested to Reilly that perhaps the United States was being overly tough with its rigorous standards. Wouldn't it be better for all concerned if the EPA just eased up a bit?

Reilly wasn't buying it. The law was there for a reason.

Then the ambassador had another idea: France will test its own wines.

Again, Reilly declined the ambassador's suggestion. But he did begin to wonder as he sat listening to the French ambassador's futile pleadings: Why isn't this chemical banned in France? How bad can it be?

Right behind the French ambassador came Italy's angry envoy. Why is the EPA making such a fuss over this? he demanded.

He left sobered when Reilly told him that procymidone in large doses had been associated with testicular cancer in rats.

Soon there were rumors that France was threatening to retaliate by blocking U.S. exports. It was beginning to look as if Reilly had fired the first shot in a full-blown trade war. Reilly sent word through the U.S. ambassador to France that this was no trade ploy, that the U.S. EPA administrator had been careful not to say "French wine could give you cancer." He promised to look for a more creative solution.

The stakes were high, and Reilly was still wondering about what he had heard from the ambassadors. They didn't dispute that the wines contained procymidone, only that they didn't understand why the United States was blocking the sale of those wines. Why would the Europeans take the huge risk of a trade war unless they thought they were on solid ground? And what were *they* doing to prevent the sales of procymidone-tainted wine at home? If the pesticide was such a threat, why would they allow it to contaminate one of their most prestigious products? He decided to do more investigating to fill in the gaps.

Reilly bore down on the data and the assumptions underlying

the concern about the effects of procymidone. He asked the experts how much contaminated wine a person would have to drink to risk a health problem.

"Two liters a day over a lifetime," they said.

Reilly couldn't believe it. "Two liters a day?! That's more than two bottles. That's what it takes to get a carcinogenic problem here? That's crazy, no one drinks two liters of wine a day."

Now it became clear to Reilly: The basis for banning procymidone was based on a very unrealistic level of consumption.

Let's rethink this, he suggested. If we assume a consumption level of two-thirds of a bottle per day—still a rather sizable amount—what would be the health risk to a person who drank that amount of wine containing minute quantities of procymidone?

"No anticipated effect," came the answer.

With that new, more realistic assumption, Reilly changed his decision. He permitted all the existing wine slated for shipment to the United States to come into the country and be sold. But he warned France, Italy, and Spain that "never again" will anything containing procymidone be allowed in.

Reilly had listened unquestioningly to his staff when he made his initial decision to ban the wine. That initial decision would have been very different had he questioned the exposure assumptions sooner. There would have been no angry confrontations with the French and Italian ambassadors and no threat of a trade war. Reilly learned a lifelong lesson from that experience.

"In today's world where managers are well educated and prepared for their jobs, they need to be more confident about asking questions and testing assumptions," he says. "If you hear something that doesn't make any sense to you and you're reasonably smart and educated and prepared for the job, then it probably doesn't make any sense, period."

Everyone from whom you seek information makes assumptions. It's up to you to find out what they are and to challenge those assumptions before making a decision based on them. It's all about analyzing the information you get from listening. Once you find out what assumptions underlie the information, ask yourself if they make sense. If they don't, find out why they don't and find out how the information would be different if the assumptions were more realistic. You may not be responsible for blocking $500 million in trade, as Reilly was, but you certainly can begin to process information the way he learned to do it.

Rule #3: Remember the Implementers

It's easy enough to listen to the people who occupy the opposite ends of any decision: the supporters and the opposers. Getting the supporters to take ownership of a decision helps build momentum and excitement and ensures that they will push implementation forward with vigor. Opposers are a little more difficult. They have a natural tendency to create obstacles to a decision and its implementation. Often, their greatest concern is that their future status will diminish because they weren't influential enough to sway the decision in their favor. But if you let them have their say early in the process, then explain clearly why you made the decision you did, even opposers will often join in backing the decision.

But what about the implementers? Implementers are the people who must execute, and they are often more junior and less influential in the organization than either supporters or op-posers. As a result, many managers make the mistake of neglect-ing the implementers, or of asking their opinions *after* a decision has already been made. Yet the implementers are the most criti-cal constituency when it comes to taking ownership of a decision and getting it done. Like everyone else, implementers want input into the decision-making process, and they will take greater own-ership when they think their voices are being heard. Conse-quently, they will work harder and drive more creative solutions to make your choice successful.

Recall Vern Loucks's Alaska invitation to 135 managers to dis-cuss whether to spin off the Caremark unit as a separate com-pany. Certainly the location was extreme, but so, too, was the number of people invited, especially when you consider that Baxter at the time had only about a dozen top managers. Loucks had purposely expanded the list of those invited to include many implementers. Because they had an early hand in the process, they became owners of the decision to split Caremark off as a separate entity. The decision met no roadblocks, and the spin-off "went smooth as silk," creating $1.5 billion in shareholder value and launching a new company that would thrive on its own.

CHAPTER 6

Be Transparent

What do you call a great decision that doesn't get executed?
Nothing but a dream.

Wise leaders know that there is far more to getting a decision executed than merely announcing it. They must also be candid and forthcoming about how and why they reached the decision. To properly carry out a decision, employees need to understand the details behind it (the good as well as the bad), why other alternatives weren't chosen, and what a realistic future holds for them if the decision is executed well or if it flops. Wise leaders tackle those issues up front, providing clear explanations about decisions and their consequences in a process we call being transparent.

To be transparent, you must first be clear about how you made your decision. It isn't necessary that the entire organization hear how and why you reached your decision, but the core team that will be in charge of making sure it gets done needs to know that you aren't making an arbitrary decision that doesn't have sound logic behind it. Telling the complete story prevents rumors and second-guessing from diverting your team's energy and efforts. If people don't know the full story, they'll fill in the gaps with rumors that are more likely to be negative than positive.

Second, be candid about the facts. A frank discussion with your team, including the data that went into making your decision, is crucial to transparency. If it's a problem you need to solve, nothing is to be gained by glossing over the severity of the problem or the consequences of not fixing it. Understanding the nature of the problem allows your team members to adjust their expectations and prepare for battle. If there's an opportunity to be seized, providing them with the facts about the value of the opportunity and the rewards it will bring the organization create enthusiasm and energy. By understanding the data that went into your decision, the team will know how you intend to measure future performance.

Finally, you need to provide your team with a road map that shows people what to do to execute your decision. They can start doing things that will be important to the new mission and stop wasting time and resources doing things that will no longer matter. Giving your team measurable milestones and a concrete goal—as well as articulating the challenges they will face—will keep them on track and help them avoid distractions that slow the pace toward the goal.

Taken together, these three facets of transparency build a foundation for execution based on trust and motivation. Transparency also has the benefit of giving your team the insights into your decision making that allow them to predict your reactions in the future and begin thinking like you think. Transparent communication isn't difficult if your decision is based on facts and sound reasoning. But it is too often neglected in the rush to get moving to execute a decision. Sharing your thinking, answering questions about your decision and how it will be executed, and conveying the urgency and seriousness will go a long way toward ensuring the fast and efficient implementation of your decision, as David Maxwell demonstrates.

SAVING THE SINKING SUBMARINE

Fannie Mae was killing itself.

Each time the company made a mortgage loan—and it made thousands each day—Fannie Mae lost more money. The drain amounted to a million dollars a day as the company staggered under the burden of $56 billion of money-losing loans.[1]

It was 1981, and David O. Maxwell had just taken over the reins as chairman of the Federal National Mortgage Association, popularly known as Fannie Mae. For years, Fannie Mae had helped people become homeowners by purchasing long term home mortgages from banks that didn't want to or couldn't afford to handle them. Fannie Mae purchased the mortgages by borrowing money short term. For years since its creation during the Depression, the business had been golden. The product was simple: plain-vanilla thirty-year mortgages. The business model was equally simple: Make money on the interest-rate "spread." That meant Fannie Mae would borrow money at low short-term rates to buy mortgages that paid higher long-term rates. It was the classic no-brainer business.

But the interest rate environment had changed radically in

the year before Maxwell took over. Inflation, fueled by skyrocketing energy costs, began to take a toll on the American economy.
The Federal Reserve, determined to crush inflation, began rais-
ing short-term interest rates, the only rates over which it had
practical control. By March 1980, it was costing Fannie Mae an
astounding 17 percent in interest to borrow short-term funds.
The mortgages it was buying typically had much-lower interest
rates. The interest-rate spread had turned negative and was
killing the company. Worse yet, Fannie Mae had committed to
continue buying mortgages for up to another year.

"As the rates went up, the mortgage bankers continued to deliver mortgages to us, and we had to borrow at the higher rates,"
Maxwell recalls. "Every mortgage that Fannie Mae had bought
since the fourth quarter of 1979 was underwater the day it hit the
books. If we continued to do business in the same way, we would
have gone broke."

Maxwell knew he had to change course, but he wasn't sure
what to do. Before making a decision, he interviewed all twenty-
six of his current executives to assess their skills and their atti-
tudes about the company. "That's when I found out how bad it
was," he says. Few of his top officers had the imagination or executive skills to change course. He immediately began replacing
many of his executives as he pondered the next step.

One solution soon became apparent: Get rid of the deadly
loans. If instead of holding the loans, Fannie Mae could package
them into securities that financial institutions would buy, the
company could make money on fees without being exposed to
the risks of fluctuating interest rates.

"We had to fashion new products that would better enable us

to match the assets and liabilities, and also to try to generate a different kind of income," he explains. "That's where the mortgage-backed securities program came in, because in that case Fannie Mae does not hold the mortgages in its portfolio, but resells them into the market and collects a fee for guaranteeing payment of the interest."

But there was a catch. To pull off Maxwell's idea, staid old Fannie Mae would have to transform itself from a passive lender to a proactive marketer. The outlook for that happening wasn't certain.

"There was no job at Fannie Mae before I got there that ever had the word *marketing* attached to it," he says. "It was just completely passive. It was like some sort of receptacle for mortgages that had become a wastepaper basket for all practical purposes given the pricing situation."

To execute the sharp change in strategy that Maxwell envisioned required that he get his staff excited about the prospect of what lay ahead, but without hiding the challenges implicit in making the transition. The first step was to summon the company's management team—still a mix of old and new—to the Wintergreen Resort in Virginia's Blue Ridge Mountains. There he explained what he intended to do. It was a mixture of cheerleading for the new strategy coupled with a stern warning that making the change wouldn't be easy. It would, he told them, "be a very tough and nerve racking next few years."

"I just wanted to make it plain to everyone that this wasn't like rolling off a log," he says. "This was going to be very difficult, and there were lots of new aspects to it, new products and new ways of marketing."

His final admonition to his troops: "Make sure you are willing to become part of this team that is going to execute this strategy and save the company!"

The reaction, he recalls, "was electric." The team seemed to be behind him and eager to take on the challenge. With one exception. After the session, one of the senior executives—a new hire, not one of the sleepy old guard—pulled Maxwell aside. "I didn't sign on for this kind of turmoil," he told Maxwell. He would be resigning as soon as they returned to the office.

The executive was a valued new leader, hired just six weeks earlier. But this was exactly why Maxwell had been so forceful and explicit in his warning about the difficulties that lay ahead. To make the changes he was envisioning, Maxwell would have no room for complainers or executives who couldn't or wouldn't pull their own weight.

"It was much better that he understood what was at stake and that he looked into his own heart and decided this atmosphere of crisis—and that's what it was going to be—was not something that he wanted to be part of," Maxwell says.

The next step was to convince Fannie Mae's board that the new way was the right way. Maxwell and his staff worked for nearly three months to develop the strategy in detail and to elaborate on some of the radical steps necessary to save the company from the death spiral in which it was trapped.

Most decisions, even big ones, typically are approved by a company's board of directors after a cursory presentation by management and a few questions and answers from directors. But Maxwell knew the changes he wanted to impose on Fannie

Mae needed more than a quick presentation. Not only were the changes a profound refocusing on Fannie Mae's business strategy, but there was also a chance they might not work! Maxwell had to show the board that he was prepared with a backup plan. In a seven-hour presentation to the board, Maxwell and his team laid out what needed to be done and some of the drastic measures that might have to be taken if Fannie Mae's cash flow didn't turn positive by specified dates. One measure was even to sell the firm's headquarters building in Washington, D.C. The time line called for the immediate sale of mortgage-backed securities to begin getting loans off the books. As for any possibility of staying the current course, the team's presentation included a chart depicting a sinking submarine headed for the bottom.

With the board's approval, Maxwell then rolled out the plan to Fannie Mae's employees, taking his show on the road to Fannie Mae's five regional offices. Again, Maxwell tried to convey not just the excitement, but also the challenges confronting the company. He set aside large amounts of time after each presentation to take questions from employees.

It took years and much effort, but eventually the new strategy was in place and working just as Maxwell had envisioned. The submarine was rising toward the surface. In 1990, the *Washingtonian* magazine marveled at the results: "David Maxwell's turnaround strategy for Fannie Mae took nearly seven years to fully implement and for investors to understand. It involved turning illiquid home mortgages into securities that institutional investors are now eager to own, gradually packaging and unloading the thousands of low-yielding mortgages the association owned, and matching Fannie Mae's assets and liabilities to pro tect itself from interest-rate fluctuations . . . under Maxwell, Fannie Mae is structured to make money, and lots of it."[2]

When David Maxwell retired from Fannie Mae in 1991, the company had gone from losing $1 million a day to earning $4 million a day.[3] The transparency that accompanied his decision to radically restructure Fannie Mae had laid the foundation for a long-term cooperative effort from all its employees to transform the company, despite the challenges confronting them.

RULES FOR BEING TRANSPARENT

Transparency is at the heart of great execution. But to be transparent requires a level of self-confidence that you can only achieve if you have been diligent about adhering to the five other principles of decision making outlined in this book. In other words, transparency is only effective if you've taken the steps necessary to be sure you're making a great decision. That isn't to say every great decision will work out the way you wish or expect. But if you have the self-confidence to be transparent, even the decisions that don't work will provide valuable lessons.

Rule #1: Be Consistent

Even the most minor actions need to be consistent with your transparent communication. It's easy to forget from time to time, but wise leaders make it a point not to. They know that any discrepancy between what you say and do will create questions about how open and honest you are. If people think you're just putting on a show instead of being transparent, any trust is impaired, if not destroyed.

Orin Smith prizes consistency. He made it a point when explaining his decisions to tie a decision back to Starbucks' six guiding principles for doing business:

- Provide a great work environment and treat each other with respect and dignity.

- Embrace diversity as an essential component in the way we do business.

- Apply the highest standards of excellence to the purchasing, roasting and fresh delivery of our coffee.

- Develop enthusiastically satisfied customers all of the time.

- Contribute positively to our communities and our environment.

- Recognize that profitability is essential to our future success.[4]

Many executives decide on a set of principles, post them somewhere, and promptly forget about them. Smith lived the principles even when it cost the company more to do that. Case in point: Starbucks' purchase of coffee beans as laid out in the principle that states the company will "apply the highest standards of excellence to the purchasing, roasting and fresh delivery of our coffee."

Starbucks has a choice when it comes to buying coffee beans. It could follow the price principle that many of its competitors use: Pay the lowest price you can; the consumer won't know it. But that wouldn't be consistent with the principle of applying the highest standards, so Starbucks *intentionally* pays more for its most important raw ingredient. It's the principle of the thing.

"We have paid prices for coffee that are based upon what we believe are the long-term interests of our farmers and our companies, and, ultimately, our shareholders," says Smith. "These prices have been, especially in the last several years, above the commodity level prices of the coffees we buy."

Is it worth it for Starbucks to pay more for coffee than it needs to in order to reinforce "the highest standards of excellence" in purchasing coffee? Smith says it is because paying more has a lot to do with how Starbucks' employees trust the company's leaders.

"The fundamental principle is, we're going to take care of our farmers, regardless of the circumstances, and we're not going to exploit them," Smith explains. "That has value in a number of ways, in terms of the long-term availability of coffee and the kind of qualities that we try to acquire. It also has a lot of value to our people, because the young people today are far more aware than their parents were of circumstances in developing countries, and they want to work for companies that treat those constituents well. How we treat our people, and how they feel about the company, is, in our view, why we're able to deliver a superior experience to the customer, relative to our competition."

For Orin Smith, it isn't enough to be consistent in *making* decisions; it's also important to be consistent in *communicating* the principles behind decisions. The truth is, Starbucks' buying practices may even save the company money. The fact that Starbucks' actions are consistent with the messages communicated in its principles solidifies employees' trust in the enterprise and increases job satisfaction. This can dramatically decrease the costs of attrition, a common problem in retail companies.

Rule #2: Dramatize Critical Decisions

When a decision will have a critical impact on your organization, it isn't always easy using just words to convey the importance of executing the decision properly. That's when wise leaders find ways to dramatize how deeply they are committed to making sure the decision is implemented. Remember from chapter 1 how Mike Ruettgers pushed EMC to develop the Symmetrix "open-storage" system long before competitors realized the market for it? The Symmetrix 3000 was, of course, a great success. But not at first.

Ruettgers had grown enormously frustrated in the weeks following the launch of the Symmetrix 3000. He knew EMC had the right product, an entirely new way for companies to store data outside of the big mainframes most were accustomed to using. He had heard hundreds of customers complain about their mainframes and the jerry-rigged ways different subsidiaries and departments had cooked up to keep their data off of mainframes and easily accessible. EMC had developed the Symmetrix 3000 to solve precisely those problems.

Based on his knowledge of the demand for a device like the Symmetrix, Ruettgers had set some ambitious sales targets embodied in the catchy phrase 2-4-8. It stood for $200 million of sales of Symmetrix systems in the first year, $400 million in the second year, and $800 million in the third year.

"I've seen goals a paragraph long, and when you ask people what the goal is, nobody can tell you," Ruettgers explains. "So I figured 2-4-8 would make it pretty simple because it was one goal, not several. It wasn't 2-4-8 with this and this and that. It was just 2-4-8."

Setting ambitious goals is one thing, but announcing those goals—especially easily remembered goals—puts a tremendous burden on a company to achieve them. But now, as the first quarter of the product launch drew to a close, the situation wasn't looking good. The company had only sold $15 million of Symmetrix systems, far below the $25 million Ruettgers had set as the target for the first quarter of the launch. Slippage, he knew, had a way of becoming a habit.

"I knew that the sales people would say, 'Hey, isn't $15 million in the first quarter a pretty good performance for a new product?' Absolutely, it probably is. But against the goal it wasn't. If we were taking this long to get going, we would never get to the $200 million goal in the first year because you'd have to make up all the shortfall and have a target in the fourth quarter of $110 million or something like that."

How to communicate his displeasure? Giving the sales force a dressing down was one option. But sales talks were old hat. Like every other sales force, EMC's salespeople had heard it all before. For years, they had been chastised, warned, praised—whatever the sales management thought would help move product. Ruettgers needed a new way to get his message across. Walking through the warehouse where hundreds of Symmetrix systems were stacked in their boxes, the idea hit him.

That night, after all the salespeople had left their offices, Ruettgers supervised a crew of forklift drivers and warehousemen that carted the boxed units from the warehouse to the administration building. There he and his crew systematically went from one sales office to the next, stacking up cartons of Symmetrix systems nearly to the ceiling. They left just enough room for the salespeople to find their desks.

The next morning, chaos reigned. But the message came through loud and clear, especially after Ruettgers ordered that the boxed systems would remain in the sales offices until delivered to paying customers. Three months later, the salespeople had clean offices and EMC was on its way to selling $800 million of the systems by 1996, far ahead of Ruettger's original target.

Rule # 3: Don't Forget the Follow-up

Transparent communication is the foundation for getting a decision executed properly. But it isn't enough to simply launch your team members toward a new goal. You have to make sure they stay on track and remain motivated. Wise leaders continue to be transparent in communicating the progress the team is making toward the goal. If hurdles arise—and they almost always do—transparent communication can identify the problem early and tap every available resource to find and implement a solution without losing momentum. This kind of communication and follow-through helped establish Harvey Golub's reputation as one of the most trusted CEOs among the investment community.

As he was driving the renewal of American Express, Golub routinely got up in front of mutual fund managers and other large shareholders to tell them why he made decisions, and what they should expect. He knew that as CEO this kind of communication with Wall Street was a big part of his job, and he took it very seriously.

What Golub didn't know was that a mutual fund manager at Fidelity Investments was writing down everything he said. "Our head of investor relations once told me that the Fidelity mutual fund manager kept track of every commitment I ever made, in any kind of speech or investor meeting," recalls Golub. The manager maintained a rigorous scrutiny of Amex's actions and checked them off as they occurred or as an explanation was given for why something didn't happen. "He once showed it to the person who is our head of investor relations," Golub says. "He showed him several pages of check marks and told him, 'When Harvey says something, you have to believe him, because look, every item is checked.'"

Golub's consistency had lasting impact. Years after Golub's retirement, Fidelity remained one of the largest shareholders of Amex stock, owning $2.6 billion in 2006.[5]

Rule #4: Conduct Postmortems

Transparency doesn't end when the execution of a decision begins. It's a continuous part of the process, even when the decision doesn't work out for the best. When well-made decisions fail, there is a reason. Perhaps a key assumption was wrong, or the market changed in an unexpected way, or a major risk was overlooked. Too often, people want to set aside the failure and channel their energy into new initiatives. But wise leaders push themselves and their organizations to figure out what went wrong. They try to be as open as possible and learn from the failure so they can better assess the risks in future decisions. They become transparent to themselves.

At Goldman Sachs, John Whitehead called his process of studying failed decisions "conducting postmortems."

"You can't underwrite a hundred IPOs in a year and not have some of them go down," he explains. "So you talk about those internally and see what went wrong and why did we not do a better job of investigating this. What did we think was going to happen and why didn't it happen, and what did we learn from it? We made a team of the people who had worked on the issue come before the management committee to explain what had gone wrong and there was an ex post facto report. We tried to learn from each of those."

Steve Schwarzman conducts a similar process at the Blackstone Group, likening failed decisions to playing basketball. "You take a jump shot. Sometimes your jump shot's working, and then sometimes you're off. The first thing you do when you're off, you say, 'What am I doing differently? How do I change this to get that ball going in the hoop again?'

"We're constantly thinking about how to make good decisions," he says. "When we don't make a good one, what did we do wrong? And what can we learn for the future? I am really fixated on that. I keep score on everything, and some people here don't like that. They think I'm second-guessing them. They don't like to confront their failures."

It is difficult to conduct the first postmortem. But once it becomes a common practice, the payback comes fast. Schwarzman says Blackstone can apply what it learns in a postmortem directly to its next deal.

"The way you see it in the subsequent experience is that when you have one of these murky decisions, you say, 'You know what? We're not going to keep to the same standard we had on the XYZ deal. We have to think about this differently.' "

For most people, a bad outcome is what results from taking an action that doesn't work out. But bad outcomes can also occur when people decide not to do something and that inaction becomes an opportunity for a competitor to seize the initiative and leap ahead. Most organizations consider errors of commission much more serious than errors of omission, but they shouldn't. Analyzing missed opportunities is just as important as analyzing failed opportunities.

While postmortems can be formal processes, as at Whitehead's Goldman Sachs, or a casual but essential part of day-to-day work, as at Blackstone, it is critical that they be action oriented and not accusatory. Effective postmortems put politics and hierarchy aside. They are, in essence, power blind. A failure by a senior member of the organization receives as thorough an investigation as one by a junior member.

But why stop at analyzing just failures? Analyzing successes—what factors went right that led to the success—is a useful exercise, especially when used to inculcate in new team members that things don't always go right, but when they do, they go right for good reasons. When conducting postmortems becomes standard practice in an organization, leaders know that risks will be better understood and decision making will continue to improve.

After all, the best long-term outcomes come from making a series of great decisions, not just one. If you are taking the right amount of risk, some decisions will work out and others won't. Wise leaders like Whitehead and Schwarzman not only take time to reflect on outcomes and articulate why decisions failed, they also use their track record of decision successes and failures to choose opportunities. They know that even if the decision fails, the lessons learned can give new direction from which their company can grow.

Practicing the Principles

The foundations for making good decisions are straightforward:

- Go to the Source.

- Fill a Room with Barbarians.

- Conquer the Fear of Risk.

- Make Vision Your Daily Guide.

- Listen with Purpose.

- Be Transparent.

Those principles are at the heart of the successes that our wise
leaders have enjoyed over the years. They are the guiding lights by
which the public company CEOs in this book drove the value of
their companies up an average of fifteen times more than the S&P
500 during their tenures.[1] They are the basis for how four of our

leaders became self-made billionaires. But as we have discovered as we try to apply them, and as you know from the stories illustrating the principles, executing them is the hard part. Following through on any single imperative with the dedication and drive that our wise leaders apply to it requires focus, effort, and time. Doing it with all six might seem impossible. Don't worry. It isn't.

Treat decision-making discipline the same way you treat your exercise discipline. Start slowly, build on each day's gains, and don't overdo it. But do it every day. That's how you build decision-making fitness and achieve business success.

The principles we outline in *How the Wise Decide* are universal and timeless. But everyone's situation is different, and there are probably some lessons that will be more useful or easier to execute in your present situation than others. Start there. If you're in sales, then going to the source is a natural place to start. You're already doing it to some extent. Use the experience of our wise leaders as a guide to do it better.

We find it useful to remember our favorite stories or rules for applying each of the principles every single day. Are you going to the source like Mike Ruettgers did to find new markets for your company or product? Are you questioning assumptions like Bill Reilly did when he discovered how the EPA set consumption levels for wine containing procymidone? Do you have a guiding vision to differentiate yourself and your company the way Dermot Dunphy differentiated Sealed Air from the rest of his industry? These real-life examples remind us that while it takes some effort to adhere to the principles, the payoffs can be huge.

As you master one principle, begin working on another. But keep all six in mind, perhaps written on an index card you carry in your pocket, because there will always be opportunities to apply them to specific decisions. Even the most cursory use of the six principles will lead to better decisions.

Keep your eyes open, too, to see if and how your colleagues are using the six principles. A colleague may exhibit the principle of seeking out dissent or embracing risk without even realizing she's doing it. Trust her judgment. If you find a colleague making decisions that aren't based on effective use of the principles, be wary. Don't hesitate to question his assumptions and methods for making decisions. Better yet, share your copy of How the Wise Decide, or at least tell him about it.

Our research to find the fundamental lessons for great decision making has been a gratifying journey. We've met remarkable leaders, all of whom have been very generous with their time and very candid about their experiences. Our website, www.wisedecide.com, is intended to be a place to learn more about decision making and the leaders we have profiled. Please join us there.

Methodology

THE METHODOLOGY BEHIND *HOW THE WISE DECIDE*

Our research began by identifying the leaders whose decisions clearly qualified them as "wise." The first step was to create a catalog of the Fortune 500 CEOs over the past thirty years. We augmented this list with individuals from Harvard Business School's 20th Century Great American Business Leaders, *Fortune*'s 50 Most Powerful Women in Business, *Forbes*'s Fab 50 companies of Asia, and our own list of the top investment firms. We then applied to the resulting list our **ESP** test:

Experience. Wisdom comes with experience, so we looked for leaders with careers spanning twenty-five years or more, and who had been the chief executive officer for at least five years.

Situations. To be great at making tough decisions, you must have had the chance to practice. We sought out leaders who were constantly placed in tough decision-making situations, such as turnarounds, periods of rapid growth, or market chaos.

Proven. Great decision making should lead to great results and respect. We wanted individuals who had consistently proven themselves over time. We looked for public-company CEOs who significantly outperformed the S&P 500 over their careers and for private-company CEOs whose organizations had enjoyed dramatic prosperity. We used *Fortune's* America's Most Admired Companies as an indicator of the respect given CEOs.

From all this emerged fifteen current and former CEOs who clearly could be called exceptional leaders.

Great leaders outside business often have valuable insight not commonly found in the corporate world. We also wanted this insight to enrich our research. So we sought out six major decision makers outside the corporate world. These include a U.S. Supreme Court justice, the prime minister of Singapore, and a Nobel laureate.

Collectively, the twenty-one wise leaders have enjoyed—and been instrumental in bringing about—tremendous success. Eight have retired as CEOs of public companies, where on average their companies outperformed the S&P 500 *by over fifteen times* when they were running them.[1] Four are self-made billionaires, and two are winners of the National Medal of Technology.

TABLE 1: The Wise

Wise Leader	Company	Position
Dermot Dunphy	Sealed Air	Chairman & CEO
Victor Fung	Li & Fung Group	Chairman
Robert Galvin	Motorola	Chairman & CEO
William George	Medtronic	Chairman & CEO
Harvey Golub	American Express	Chairman & CEO
William Hearst III	Kleiner Perkins Caufield & Byers	General Partner
Shelly Lazarus	Ogilvy & Mather Worldwide	Chairman & CEO
Vernon Loucks	Baxter International	Chairman & CEO
David Maxwell	Fannie Mae	Chairman & CEO
Peter Peterson	Lehman Brothers	Chairman & CEO
Michael Ruettgers	EMC	CFO
Stephen Schwarzman	The Blackstone Group	CEO
Orin Smith	Starbucks	CEO
Richard Wagoner	General Motors	Chairman & CEO
John Whitehead	Goldman Sachs	Cochairman

Wise Leader	Organization	Position
Stephen Breyer	U.S. Supreme Court	Associate Justice
Daniel Kahneman	Princeton University	Nobel Prize– winning professor
Dean Kamen	DEKA Research & Development	Founder & CEO
Lee Hsien Loong	Singapore	Prime Minister Deputy Prime Minister
William Reilly	World Wildlife Fund Environmental Protection Agency	Chairman Administrator
Lawrence Summers	Harvard University U.S. Department of the Treasury	President Secretary

Once we had our list of wise leaders, we began the process of analyzing how they make tough decisions. Our research consisted of three steps.

Discussing Tough Decisions

Early on, a Harvard expert in decision theory gave us a piece of advice that stuck with us: 90 perent of the value a leader provides comes from the most important and challenging 10 percent of his or her decisions. Using this benchmark, we focused our initial research interviews with the wise leaders on the toughest decisions they had made in their careers. For example, Harvey Golub explained why he spun off Shearson Lehman into a separate company immediately after he took over as CEO of American Express, and Rick Wagoner discussed making the choice to shut down Oldsmobile.

Distilling the Principles

Next, we sifted through more than a thousand pages of transcripts of our interviews, looking for overarching patterns inherent in the decisions the leaders described. Every time we identified a theme, we wrote it on a Post-it note and grouped the notes on the wall by topic.

Months later, multiple walls were covered with yellow Post-its highlighting over a hundred distinct ideas about decision making. We reorganized constantly to place similar and reinforcing ideas next to one another. We then distilled these clusters of ideas into dozens of lessons, and finally grouped these lessons into the six universal principles—each a composite of insights from our wise leaders—that provide the backbone of this book.

Making the Principles Practical

To ensure that the six principles were applicable to our readers' experience, we went back to many of the wise leaders to drill down for takeaway advice. We asked questions such as "What did you do to get comfortable with taking such risks?" and "What did you say to the person who opposed your decision?" We also tested our findings with colleagues to ensure that our advice would help them make wise decisions as managers. It is these takeaways that became the rules for the practicable application of each principle in your own job.

Peer Survey

We surveyed one hundred of our peers to see if they felt a need equal to ours for decision-making guidance. They did. In the survey of one hundred MBAs from top programs and corporate managers, we presented each individual with a fictitious situation in which he or she ran a small company. Then we asked them how qualified they felt to make thirteen common but significant business decisions, such as hiring a law firm, approving a marketing campaign, and setting a strategic direction. The results were powerful. For only two of the thirteen decisions did more than 60 percent of respondents feel qualified to make the decision. More important, in five of the thirteen decisions, fewer than 40 percent of respondents felt qualified to make the decision. These managers clearly did not feel prepared, either. Their insights helped us to focus our questions and make our case to the targeted participants.

SURVEY QUESTION

Suppose you started a new company tomorrow and had to make the following decisions as you launched your business. How qualified are you to make each decision?

Percent Responding "Extremely Qualified" or "Qualified"

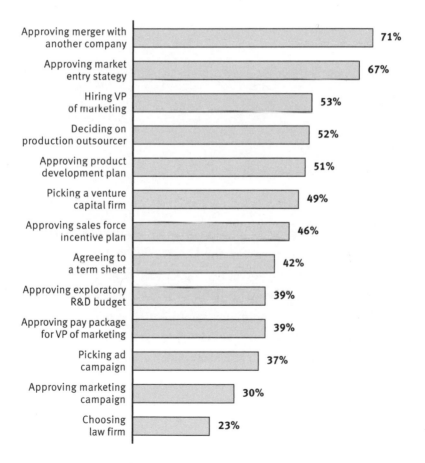

Decision	Percent
Approving merger with another company	71%
Approving market entry stategy	67%
Hiring VP of marketing	53%
Deciding on production outsourcer	52%
Approving product development plan	51%
Picking a venture capital firm	49%
Approving sales force incentive plan	46%
Agreeing to a term sheet	42%
Approving exploratory R&D budget	39%
Approving pay package for VP of marketing	39%
Picking ad campaign	37%
Approving marketing campaign	30%
Choosing law firm	23%

Leader Profiles

Stephen Breyer

U.S. Supreme Court Associate Justice

Stephen Breyer has been an associate justice on the United States Supreme Court since 1994. Before serving on the U.S. Supreme Court, Justice Breyer was on the U.S. Court of Appeals for the First Circuit, where he served as chief judge from 1990 to 1994. Justice Breyer was a member of the Harvard Law School faculty from 1967 to 1980, receiving appointment to professor in 1970. He was also a professor at Harvard University's Kennedy School of Government from 1977 to 1980, and a lecturer at Harvard Law School from 1981 to 1994. Justice Breyer served as a clerk for the Honorable Arthur J. Goldberg of the U.S. Supreme Court, as assistant special prosecutor in the Watergate investigation, and as chief counsel of the Senate Judiciary Committee.

T. J. Dermot Dunphy

Former Chairman and Chief Executive Officer, Sealed Air

T. J. Dermot Dunphy was chairman and CEO of Sealed Air from 1971 to 2000. During this time, Sealed Air grew from a $5 million packaging company to a $3 billion Fortune 500 business with sixty plants operating around the world. Mr. Dunphy began his career at Westinghouse Electric in 1956. He left Westinghouse to become the president of Custom-Made Packaging, which he later sold to Hammermill in 1968. In 1971, he was asked by his business school friends, the founders of Wall Street firm Donaldson Lufkin & Jenrette (DLJ), to take over as head of Sealed Air. He retired as chairman in 2000 and currently serves as chairman of Kildare Enterprises, a private-equity firm headquartered in New Jersey. He has received an Alumni Achievement Award from Harvard Business School.

Dr. Victor K. Fung

Chairman, Li & Fung Group

Dr. Victor Fung is the group chairman of the Li & Fung Group of companies, which includes major subsidiaries in trading, distribution, and retailing, including publicly listed Li & Fung Limited, Integrated Distribution Services Group Limited, and Convenience Retail Asia. Li & Fung Group operates in more than forty countries and trades more than $10 billion in merchandise annually. Dr. Fung, who received his Ph.D. from Harvard Business School, is currently chairman of the Greater Pearl River Delta

Business Council, the Hong Kong Airport Authority, the Hong Kong University Council, and the Hong Kong–Japan Business Co-operation Committee. Dr. Fung holds a number of civic and professional appointments. He is a member of the Chinese People's Political Consultative Conference and the Hong Kong Government Judicial Officers Recommendation Committee. From 1991 to 2000, Dr. Fung was chairman of the Hong Kong Trade Development Council, and from 1996 to 2003, he was the Hong Kong representative on the APEC Business Advisory Council. In 2003, the government awarded Dr. Fung the Gold Bauhinia Star for distinguished service to the community.

Robert Galvin

Former Chairman and Chief Executive Officer, Motorola

Robert Galvin was chairman and CEO of Motorola from 1958 to 1986. Under Mr. Galvin's leadership, Motorola sales increased from $216.6 million to $6.7 billion, and cash flow per share grew from 89 cents to $6.10. Mr. Galvin started his career at Motorola in 1940. He was named president of the company in 1956 and succeeded his father, Paul Galvin, as the CEO in 1958. In 1986, Mr. Galvin gave up the title of CEO while remaining chairman of the board. In 1990, he became chairman of the Executive Committee. In 1991, Mr. Galvin published *The Idea of Ideas,* presenting a variety of ideas that influenced his ability to lead Motorola through more than three decades. He has received honorary degrees and numerous awards, including election to the National Business Hall of Fame and the presentation of the

National Medal of Technology in 1991. Motorola was the first large company-wide winner of the Malcolm Baldridge National Quality Award, presented to Mr. Galvin by President Ronald Reagan.

William George

Former Chairman and Chief Executive Officer, Medtronic

William George was chairman and CEO of Medtronic, Inc., from 1991 to 2001. Under his leadership, the company's market capitalization grew from $1.1 billion to $60 billion, averaging 35 percent growth per year. Mr. George joined Medtronic in 1989 as president and chief operating officer. He was a member of the Medtronic board from 1989 to 2002, serving as its chairman from 1996 to 2002. Prior to joining Medtronic, Mr. George served in executive positions at Honeywell and Litton Industries, and as a civilian in the U.S. Department of Navy. Mr. George currently is a director of Goldman Sachs, Novartis, and ExxonMobil. He is also a member of numerous nonprofit boards, including Harvard Business School, the Minneapolis Institute of Arts, and the Carnegie Endowment for International Peace. Mr. George is the author of *Authentic Leadership: Rediscovering the Secrets to Create Lasting Value* and *True North: Discover Your Authentic Leadership.* Mr. George was named one of the "25 Most Influential Business People of the Last 25 Years" by PBS Nightly News. He has received a Legend in Leadership Award from Yale University.

Harvey Golub
Former Chairman and Chief Executive Officer, American Express
  Company

Harvey Golub was chairman and CEO of American Express from 1993 to 2001. In 1984, Mr. Golub joined American Express as president and CEO of IDS Financial Services, as a member of American Express's board of directors, and was elected vice chairman of American Express. He was named president of American Express in 1991 and named chairman and CEO of American Express Travel Related Services later that year. Prior to joining American Express, Mr. Golub was a senior partner with McKinsey & Company. Mr. Golub currently serves as chairman of Campbell Soup Company. In addition, he served as a member or chairman of Warnaco's board and on the boards of other private companies. He currently is executive chairman of Ripplewood Holdings, a private-equity firm headquartered in New York. He also serves on the nonprofit boards of Lincoln Center, the American Enterprise Institute, and New York–Presbyterian Hospital. Mr. Golub has been listed in *Forbes*'s "America's Most Powerful People."

William R. Hearst III
Affiliated Partner, Kleiner Perkins Caufield & Byers
Former General Partner, Kleiner Perkins Caufield & Byers

William R. Hearst III joined venture capital firm Kleiner Perkins Caufield & Byers in January 1995 and currently serves on the boards of Akimbo, Applied Minds, Juniper Networks, Oblix, On-Fiber, and RGB Networks. In addition to his portfolio company boards, he is also a director of the Hearst Corporation and Hearst-Argyle Television. Hearst is a fellow of the American Association for the Advancement of Science and a trustee of The Hearst Foundation, Carnegie Institution of Washington, Mathematical Sciences Research Institute, California Academy of Sciences, and Grace Cathedral in San Francisco. Hearst was editor and publisher of the *San Francisco Examiner* from 1984 until 1995.

Daniel Kahneman

Nobel Prize Winner, Economics, 2002

Eugene Higgins Professor of Psychology, Princeton University, and Professor of Public Affairs, Woodrow Wilson School

Daniel Kahneman is a Nobel laureate and the Eugene Higgins Professor of Psychology at Princeton University and professor of psychology and public affairs at its Woodrow Wilson School. Professor Kahneman is the second psychologist to win the Nobel Prize, and the first with a pure psychology background. Prospect theory, for which Professor Kahneman was awarded the prize, challenges mainstream economists' assumptions that people are rational and motivated by self-interest when making financial decisions. Instead, Kahneman suggested that psychological motives, including emotions and biases, influence economic behavior, causing people to make flawed but human choices when making financial decisions. Before joining the Princeton faculty in 1993, Professor Kahneman was a professor at the Hebrew University, the University of British Columbia, and the University of California, Berkeley. Professor Kahneman has received numerous awards in the psychology field, including the Hilgard Award for Distinguished Contribution to General Psychology, the Warren Medal of the Society of Experimental Psychologists, the Distinguished Scientific Contribution Award from the American Psychological Association, and the Grawemeyer Award for Psychology.

Dean Kamen

Founder and Chief Executive Officer, DEKA Research & Development
  Corporation
Founder, FIRST (For Inspiration and Recognition of Science and
  Technology)

Dean Kamen is an inventor, an entrepreneur, and an advocate for science and technology. Mr. Kamen is the founder and president of DEKA Research & Development Corporation and the founder of FIRST (For Inspiration and Recognition of Science and Technology), a nonprofit organization whose mission is to motivate the next generation to want to learn about science and technology. As an inventor, he holds more than 150 U.S. and foreign patents, many of them for innovative medical devices. Prior to founding DEKA and FIRST, Mr. Kamen founded and ran AutoSyringe, a company based on medical technology he developed while an undergraduate. Mr. Kamen's honors include the Kilby Award, which celebrates those who make extraordinary contributions to society; the Heinz Award in Technology, the Economy, and Employment; and the National Medal of Technology, awarded by President Clinton in 2000 for "inventions that have advanced medical care worldwide and for innovative and imaginative leadership in awakening America to the excitement of science and technology."

Rochelle (Shelly) Lazarus
Chairman and CEO, Ogilvy & Mather Worldwide

Chief executive of advertising giant Ogilvy since 1996, Lazarus started at the company more than thirty years ago while founder David Ogilvy was still walking the halls. Thanks to her vision, Ogilvy boasts some of the world's most recognizable, and profitable, clients, including American Express, Kodak, Motorola, IBM, Kraft, and DuPont. Lazarus serves on several notable boards, including General Electric and Merck.

Lee Hsien Loong
Prime Minister, Singapore

Lee Hsien Loong has been Singapore's third prime minister since 2004. Since he was first elected to Parliament in 1984, he has held ministerial appointments in Trade and Industry, Defense, and Finance. In the economic ministries, he has pursued policies to promote growth, by fostering a pro-market business climate and light taxes. Mr. Lee has also been chairman of the Monetary Authority of Singapore (MAS), where he liberalized the financial sector and shifted the emphasis from one-size-fits-all regulation toward a lighter supervisory touch. Before becoming prime minister, Mr. Lee was deputy prime minister for fourteen years, with responsibility for economic and civil-service matters.

As prime minister, Mr. Lee has launched policies to build a competitive economy and an inclusive society. Mr. Lee's government is also strengthening Singapore's social safety nets. Significant measures include the Workfare Incentive Scheme, which is a negative income tax to encourage and reward older, low-income workers, and Community Care (ComCare), an endowment fund to support a wide range of welfare and social programs targeted at the poor. One ongoing major project is reform of the Central Provident Fund (CPF) system, a fully funded social security and pension scheme based on compulsory personal savings accounts, to cope with lengthening life spans.

Before entering politics, Mr. Lee was a brigadier-general in the Singapore Armed Forces (SAF). He attended the U.S. Army Command and General Staff College at Fort Leavenworth, Kansas, and held various staff and command posts.

Vernon R. Loucks Jr.

Former Chairman and Chief Executive Officer, Baxter International

Vernon R. Loucks Jr. was CEO of Baxter International from 1980 through 1998, and chairman of the board from 1987 through 1999. He joined Baxter in 1966 as assistant to the CEO. His career at Baxter included senior positions in both domestic and U.S. operations. In 1975, he was elected to the company's board and became president and COO in 1976. Mr. Loucks currently serves on the boards of Affymetrix, Anheuser-Busch Companies, Edwards Lifesciences, Emerson Electric, and MedAssets, Inc. He is a member of the Council of Retired Chief Executives, is former chairman and co-founder of the Healthcare Leadership Council, and served as special adviser to the U.S. National Institutes of Health. Mr. Loucks received the Yale Medal and the William McCormick Blair Award from Yale University.

David O. Maxwell

Retired Chairman and Chief Executive Officer, Fannie Mae

David O. Maxwell was the chairman and CEO of Fannie Mae from 1981 to 1991. Prior to leading Fannie Mae, Mr. Maxwell served as CEO of Ticor Mortgage Insurance. He was a lawyer in Philadelphia and served as an officer in the U.S. Navy. He is a trustee emeritus of the National Gallery of Art, an honorary trustee of the Brookings Institution, and vice president of the Jovid Foundation. Mr. Maxwell was named one of "The 10 Greatest CEOs of All Time" by *Fortune* magazine in 2003.

Peter G. Peterson

Senior Chairman and Cofounder, The Blackstone Group
Former Chairman and Chief Executive Officer, Lehman Brothers
Former U.S. Secretary of Commerce
Former Chairman and Chief Executive Officer, Bell and Howell
  Corporation

Peter G. Peterson is the senior chairman of The Blackstone Group, a private-equity firm he cofounded in 1985. Prior to founding Blackstone, Mr. Peterson was chairman and CEO of Lehman Brothers from 1973 to 1977, and after the merger with Kuhn, Loeb he became chairman and CEO of Lehman Brothers, Kuhn, Loeb, Inc., from 1977 to 1984. He served as secretary of commerce under President Nixon from 1972 to 1973. He was also chairman and CEO of Bell and Howell from 1963 to 1971. He is the founding president of the Concord Coalition and has formerly served as a director of Sony Corporation, 3M Company, Federated Department Stores, Black & Decker, General Foods, RCA, the Continental Group, and Cities Services. He has received a number of awards, including a U.S. Junior Chamber of Commerce award naming him one of the "Ten Outstanding Men" in the nation. In 1962, *Life* magazine cited him as one of the one hundred most important Americans under forty. He has also received the University of Chicago Alumni Medal (its highest honor) and honorary degrees from Colgate University, Georgetown University, George Washington University, and Northwestern University, among others. He was declared a Living Legend by the New York Historical Society in November 2003.

William K. Reilly

Former Administrator, U.S. Environmental Protection Agency
Chairman Emeritus and Former President, World Wildlife Fund

William K. Reilly served as administrator of the U.S. Environmental Protection Agency from 1989 to 1993, directing eighteen thousand employees and a $7 billion budget. During his time at the EPA, Mr. Reilly played a pivotal role in crafting and securing passage of a new Clean Air bill, enacted by Congress and signed into law by President George H. W. Bush in 1990. Mr. Reilly is chairman emeritus of the board of the World Wildlife Fund and is a founding partner of Aqua International, LP, a private-equity fund dedicated to investing in companies engaged in water and renewable energy, and a senior adviser to TPG Capital, LP. Prior to serving at the EPA, Mr. Reilly was the president of the World Wildlife Fund, and before that the president of the Conservation Foundation. Mr. Reilly is a director of DuPont, ConocoPhillips, and Royal Caribbean International. He is also a director of the National Geographic Society and the Packard Foundation.

Michael C. Ruettgers

Former Chairman and Chief Executive Officer, EMC Corporation

Michael C. Ruettgers was CEO of EMC Corporation from 1992 to 2001, and executive chairman of EMC's board from 2000 to 2003. Mr. Ruettgers joined EMC in 1988. From his arrival through year-end 2000, EMC's revenues grew from $120 million to nearly $9 billion. Mr. Ruettgers became chairman of the board in 2004 and retired from EMC at the end of 2007. During the ten-year bull market from October 1990 to October 2000, EMC achieved the highest single-decade performance of any listed stock in the history of the New York Stock Exchange. Prior to joining EMC, Mr. Ruettgers spent much of his early career with Raytheon, where he played a key role in the Patriot missile program. Mr. Ruettgers was named one of the "Best CEOs in America" by *Worth* magazine and was inducted into the IT Industry Hall of Fame in 2002.

Stephen A. Schwarzman

Chairman, Chief Executive Officer, and Cofounder,
The Blackstone Group

Stephen Schwarzman is the chairman and CEO of The Blackstone Group, a private-equity firm he cofounded in 1985. Mr. Schwarzman began his career at Lehman Brothers, where he was elected managing director in 1978 at the age of thirty-one. He served as chairman of the firm's Mergers and Acquisitions group from 1983 to 1984. Mr. Schwarzman is chairman of the board of the John F. Kennedy Center for the Performing Arts and served as an adjunct professor at the Yale School of Management. He is on the boards of many organizations, including the New York Public Library, the New York City Ballet, the Frick Collection, the Asia Society, and the New York City Partnership.

Orin C. Smith
Former President and Chief Executive Officer, Starbucks Coffee

Orin C. Smith is the recently retired CEO and president of Starbucks. Mr. Smith joined Starbucks in 1990 as the company's CFO. He was president and COO from 1994 to 2000 and was appointed CEO in 2000. Prior to serving at Starbucks, Mr. Smith was CFO of two transportation companies and spent fourteen years at Deloitte & Touche. He has served as chief policy and finance adviser in the administration of two Washington State governors. Mr. Smith serves on the board of Nike, The Walt Disney Company, and Washington Mutual. In 2002, Mr. Smith received an Alumni Achievement Award from Harvard Business School.

Lawrence H. Summers
Charles W. Eliot University Professor, Harvard University
Managing Director, D. E. Shaw Group
Former President, Harvard University
Former U.S. Secretary of the Treasury

Lawrence H. Summers is Charles Eliot University Professor at Harvard University and managing director of D. E. Shaw Group, a $25 billion hedge fund. From 2001 to 2006, Summers was the twenty-seventh president of Harvard University. Prior to his appointment at Harvard, Mr. Summers was secretary of the treasury under President Clinton from 1999 to 2001. In that capacity, he served as the principal economic adviser to the president and as the CFO of the U.S. government, with a civilian workforce of

150,000. Mr. Summers's prior experience includes roles as under-secretary of the Treasury under Robert Rubin, vice president of development economics and chief economist of the World Bank, and professor of economics at Harvard University, where he was one of the youngest individuals in recent history to receive tenure. He is the first social scientist ever to receive the Alan T. Waterman Award of the National Science Foundation, established by Congress to honor an exceptional U.S. scientist or engineer, and was awarded the John Bates Clark Medal, given every two years to an outstanding American economist under the age of forty. Mr. Summers also received the Alexander Hamilton Medal, the Treasury Department's highest honor. *Time* named Summers one of the one hundred most influential people in the world in 2005.

G. Richard Wagoner

Chairman and Chief Executive Officer, General Motors

G. Richard Wagoner is chairman and CEO of General Motors. Mr. Wagoner began his GM career in 1977 as an analyst in the treasurer's office in New York. He was CFO from 1992 to 1994, EVP and president of North American Operations from 1994 to 1998, and president and COO from 1998 to 2000. Mr. Wagoner also held a number of executive positions in GM's international operations, including General Motors of Brazil, General Motors of Canada, and General Motors Europe. Mr. Wagoner serves as chairman of the Board of Visitors for Duke University's Fuqua School of Business. He has received an Alumni Achievement Award from Harvard Business School.

John C. Whitehead

Chairman, Goldman Sachs Foundation
Chairman, AEA Investors
Former U.S. Deputy Secretary of State
Former Cochairman, Goldman Sachs

John C. Whitehead is chairman of the Goldman Sachs Foundation and of AEA Investors. Mr. Whitehead began his career at Goldman, Sachs & Company, where he worked for thirty-eight years, becoming a partner in 1956 and cochairman of the firm in 1976. During Mr. Whitehead's tenure, Goldman Sachs became one of the world's preeminent investment banks. Mr. Whitehead retired from Goldman Sachs in 1984. In 1985, President Reagan appointed Mr. Whitehead deputy secretary of state under George Schultz, where he was instrumental in major diplomatic initiatives, including NATO expansion in central and eastern Europe. Mr. Whitehead served in the U.S. Navy during World War II, participating in the invasions of Normandy, Iwo Jima, and Okinawa. Mr. Whitehead has served as chairman of the board of directors of the Federal Reserve Bank of New York, the International Rescue Committee, the Asia Society, the Andrew W. Mellon Foundation, the Harvard Board of Overseers, and the Haverford Board of Managers. Mr. Whitehead was awarded the Presidential Citizens Medal by President Reagan and was honored by the Aspen Institute with its 2002 Corporate Leadership Award.

The 21 Club

1. Lisa Endlich, *Goldman Sachs: The Culture of Success* (New York: Alfred A. Knopf, 1999), 81.
2. *The 1992 Innovation Survey,* Group EFO Limited; Dan Lovallo and Daniel Kahneman, "Delusions of Success" *Harvard Business Review,* July 2003, 4.
3. Meeting with Glenn Hubbard, 6/22/04.

1. Go to the Source

1. From Bill George's True North website, www.truenorthleaders.com.
2. Starbucks Corporation, *10k,* 1999.
3. "Trouble Brewing," *Newsweek,* July 19, 1999.
4. Performance is based on adjusted share prices from January 1, 1990, to December 31, 1999, as reported by Yahoo! Finance.
5. John Whitehead, *A Life In Leadership* (New York: Basic Books, 2005), 120.
6. Ibid.
7. Ibid.
8. *Yarborough v. Alvarado,* 541 U.S. 652 (2004).

2. Fill a Room with Barbarians

1. "An Evolutionary Approach to Revolutionary Change," *Human Resource Planning,* June 1994.
2. *The Evolution of Six Sigma,* Process Quality Associates Inc. website, November 13, 2007.

3. "Motorola: In Search of Perfection," *PC Communications* 4, no. 3, March 1993.

4. Robert W. Rubin and Jacob Weisberg, *In an Uncertain World* (New York: Random House, 2003), 14.

5. Ibid., 23–24.

6. Ibid., 23.

7. Ibid., 24.

8. Ibid., 23, 34. Public accounts differ on the total amount of the aid package, as many include (in Rubin's words) "short-term contributions from the Bank for International Settlements that Mexico couldn't practically use to pay off Tesobono holders or finance imports." The *International Herald Tribune* reports $53 billion—see www.iht.com/articles/1995/02/17/peso_5.php.

3. Conquer the Fear of Risk

1. D. Kahneman, and A. Tversky, "Prospect Theory: An Analysis of Decisions under Risk," *Econometrica* 47 (1979).

2. "50 Most Powerful Women in Business 2007," *Fortune* company website, November 13, 2007.

3. "Research Brief: Asbestos Litigation Costs, Compensation, and Alternatives," RAND Corporation website, November 13, 2007.

4. According to Blackstone company website, as of December 31, 2007.

5. *The Blackstone Group 20 Years* (New York: Newmarket Publishing and Communications Company), 26.

6. Shelly Lazarus biography on www.answers.com.

4. Make Vision Your Daily Guide

1. Dunphy interview with Harvard Business School, 6.

2. Ibid., 8.

3. Ibid.

4. Ibid., 13.

5. Sealed Air press release, January 25, 2001, http://ir.sealedair.com /releasedetail.cfm?releaseid=74113; Dunphy interview, 13.

6. Sealed Air press release, October 25, 1999, http://ir.sealedair.com /ReleaseDetail.cfm?ReleaseID=74279.

7. Company return is based on the closing price adjusted for splits and dividends on January 1 of the first year as CEO and December 31 of the last year as CEO as reported by Historical Quotes on Yahoo!

5. Listen with Purpose

1. HBS case study "Baxter Healthcare Corporation: ASAP Express," February 11, 1991, 1.

2. http://www.ncbi.nlm.nih.gov/pubmed/10282373.

3. *Straits Times*, Insight Survey, August 11, 2007.

4. See www.cpf.gov.sg (Singapore Government Central Provident Fund website).

5. The Status of Wild Atlantic Salmon: A River by River Assessment, World Wildlife Fund.

6. "Goodbye to Dad's Olds," *CNNMoney*, December 12, 2000.

7. Ibid.

8. "End of the Road for Olds," *CNNMoney*, December 12, 2000.

9. "Goodbye to Dad's Olds."

6. Be Transparent

1. "Good to Great," *Fast Company*, September 2001.

2. "Businessman of the Year," *Washingtonian*, July 1990.

3. "Good to Great."

4. Starbucks company website, 2006.

5. Yahoo! Finance.

Practicing the Principles

1. Company return is based on the closing price adjusted for splits and dividends on January 1 of the first year as CEO and December 31 of the last year as CEO as reported by Historical Quotes on Yahoo! Sealed Air went public in 1979; however, adjusted data only exist from 1988. Bob Galvin's tenure spanned 1958 to 1986; however, adjusted data only exists back to 1977. Peter Peterson was CEO of Bell and Howell from 1963 to 1971. Historical data is not available for that period. Orin Smith could not be included because the S&P 500 had a negative performance during this period, making a ratio meaningless. The measurement period ended on March 31, 2005.

Appendix A: Methodology

1. Company return is based on the closing price adjusted for splits and dividends on January 1 of the first year as CEO and December 31 of the last year as CEO as reported by Historical Quotes on Yahoo! Sealed Air went public in 1979; however, adjusted data only exist from 1988. Bob Galvin's tenure spanned 1958 to 1986; however, adjusted data only exists back to 1977. Peter Peterson was CEO of Bell and Howell from 1963 to 1971. Historical data is not available for that period. Orin Smith could not be included because the S&P 500 had a negative performance during this period, making a ratio meaningless. The measurement period ended on March 31, 2005.

ACKNOWLEDGMENTS

This book would not be possible without the time, energy, and insights of the twenty-one wise leaders. We are deeply grateful to them.

Our thanks to Ike Williams of Kneerim & Williams and John Mahaney of Crown Business for believing in this book, and to Doug Sease for his talent, patience, and flair.

Richard Zeckhauser provided invaluable guidance and help at many stages of our research and writing. Sarah Sandoski provided essential support to our research. We owe an enormous debt to them.

We are also grateful to the Ewing Marion Kauffman Foundation for its financial support of the project. A group of insightful and distinguished individuals provided guidance when we were getting started, including Glenn Hubbard of Columbia Business School and Howard Raiffa, Clay Christensen, Michael Wheeler, Nancy Koehn, and Bill Sahlman of Harvard Business School. We appreciate their direction. Thanks also to the friends and colleagues who reviewed early manuscripts, including Alex Kinnier, Michael Monson, Alex Saltonstall, Laura Saltonstall, Tripp Jones, Dan Jones, and Chris Choi. We are grateful to Hope

Denekamp, Stacy Ferguson, Lindsay Orman, Gillian Blake, and Miriam Avins for their help along the way.

Finally, thank you to our spouses, Maribel Sandoski and Clift Jones, who believed in and supported this project more than anyone. Our wisest decisions were to marry the two of you.

INDEX

ABOUT THE AUTHORS

AARON SANDOSKI is cofounder and managing director of Norwich Ventures, a specialized venture capital firm focusing on early-stage medical device investing. He regularly uses the principles of *How the Wise Decide* to make investment decisions and help his portfolio companies make operational and strategic decisions. Aaron began his professional career as a management consultant at McKinsey & Company and has worked at a number of start-up companies throughout the past decade.

Aaron received a double BA in economics and chemistry from Dartmouth College, where he graduated summa cum laude, and an MBA from Harvard Business School. As a Teaching Fellow at Harvard University in 2003, he taught introductory micro and macro economics and won the Allyn Young Teaching Prize.

BRYN ZECKHAUSER is a principal at Equity Resource Investments, a firm that invests in real estate in the United States and Asia, and a Senior Fellow at Harvard University's Mossavar-Rahmani Center for Business and Government. She developed her interest in strategic decision making working with portfolio companies at Kleiner Perkins Caufield & Byers and with her Fortune 500 clients at McKinsey & Company.

Bryn received a BA in economics magna cum laude from Harvard College and an MBA with distinction from Harvard Business School, where she was awarded the Robert Jasse Award for leadership and entrepreneurship.